T0374201

A DEEPER WALK IN GOD'S LOVE

Dottie Burdette

WESTBOW
PRESS®
A DIVISION OF THOMAS NELSON
& ZONDERVAN

WestBow Press books may be ordered through booksellers or by contacting:

WestBow Press
A Division of Thomas Nelson & Zondervan
1663 Liberty Drive
Bloomington, IN 47403
www.westbowpress.com
844-714-3454

Scripture marked (NKJV) taken from the New King James Version®. Copyright © 1982 by Thomas Nelson. Used by permission. All rights reserved.

Scripture quotations marked (NIV) are taken from the Holy Bible, New International Version®, NIV®. Copyright © 1973, 1978, 1984, 2011 by Biblica, Inc.® Used by permission of Zondervan. All rights reserved worldwide. www.zondervan.com The "NIV" and "New International Version" are trademarks registered in the United States Patent and Trademark Office by Biblica, Inc.®

ISBN: 978-1-6642-6730-5 (sc)
ISBN: 978-1-6642-6731-2 (hc)
ISBN: 978-1-6642-6729-9 (e)

Library of Congress Control Number: 2022909604

Print information available on the last page.

WestBow Press rev. date: 06/24/2022

This is the second book that I believe God has asked me to write. As you read it, you may find some writings shadow those found in my first book, *Tidbits of God's Love.* As was *Tidbits,* this book was written with love for our Lord and His children as well.

And once again, should someone be touched by something found between these covers, by some of the words on these pages, my prayers will be answered. My sincere desire is to share the things of God I see, things I believe God shares with me – and has asked me to share with you.

And I give all the glory to our Lord for allowing me to work for Him in this compacity.

So please, enjoy.

Dottie

Lord, Why Am I Writing?

So, Lord, why am I writing such things? You are filling my mind with ideas and stories. Sometimes more that I can remember. So much so that at times I must write them down or I will forget them. And oh, how I want to remember what you have shown me.

I feel compelled to write down the things you show me—the things you tell me—through daily quiet time, through prayer time, and through your Word. I feel I must share them with anyone who will give me half an ear. I cannot help it. It just happens. I need to do this almost as much as I need to eat or sleep or breathe. I can fully relate to Jeremiah when he said that God's word was like fire in his bones, and he could no longer hold it in.

So why am I doing this? Since the Lord will answer our questions with His Word, let us turn to the Bible.

> Each one should use whatever gift he has received to serve others, faithfully administering God's grace in its various forms. If anyone speaks, he should to it as one speaking the very words of God. If anyone serves, he should do it with the strength God provides, so that in all things God may be praised through Jesus Christ. To him be the glory and the power for ever an ever. Amen.
>
> (1 Peter 4:10–11 NIV)

Ah! There it is. The Lord Himself—the maker of

heaven and earth—has given me a gift that I am to share with my body of believers, my Christian family. I did not see anything about being a best-selling author or a well-known writer. Nor did I see anything about getting paid for this service. What I <u>did</u> see was the Lord telling me that the gifts we have are gifts that He has given us. And that these gifts are not just for us alone, but for others as well. God gave us these gifts not so we could become rich or famous, but so we could serve others.

I also see that God gives each one of us gifts. Yes! God gave you gifts too. Maybe not the gift of gab as I seem to have, but gifts of your own. Perhaps your gift is serving others. Maybe it is in leadership. Singing. Playing music. Writing poems. Creating beautiful paintings. Organization. Decorating. Cooking. I could go on.

God gave us the gifts He wanted us to have and use. We are not to just sit on them or hide them in a closet; we are to use them, develop them, enjoy them, and share them with the body of Christ. With our church family. Our coworkers. Family members. Grocery store clerks. Doctors. Any and everyone who looks as if our gifts could help them. Each one should use whatever gift he or she has received to serve others. Faithfully administering God's grace in its various forms is what we are told to do in 1 Peter 4.

We are to share our gifts for two reasons. First, collectively, the church—you and me—equals one body. There are different parts to our biological bodies, and there are different gifts in our church body. Our biological bodies are healthier when all the different parts work well, and our church bodies are healthier when all the gifts are shared.

But second and perhaps a tad more important, when

we use our gifts to serve others, we are being obedient to God, who asked us to use them and to give them away. And I know we all want to honor the Father's wishes by being obedient and doing as He has asked.

So, use your gift as a form of worship back to our Lord. Enjoy it. Allow it to fill your soul. To enlighten your world. I cannot help but to think that when we do, our Lord smiles.

A Special Resurrection

I have struggled for the past few days with the next verses in Proverbs 3 that we are to study, but I believe the Lord has asked me to veer away from them just for this week. This is Resurrection Sunday, Easter, a special day for Christians, those who belong to God's family, those who have God's seal of ownership and His spirit in their hearts.

> Now it is God who makes both us and you stand firm in Christ. He anointed us, set his seal of ownership on us, and put his Spirit in our hearts as a deposit, guaranteeing what is to come. (2 Corinthians 1:21 NIV)

This is the day of our Savior's resurrection. The day the Messiah became our redeemer. The day God showed the Pharisees, the Roman soldiers, and those who wanted to kill Jesus that He was much more than the mere mortal man they thought He was. The day when Jesus confirmed all He had told His disciples about—that He was going to suffer greatly, die, and come back to life.

And then He did just that. He suffered scourging, beatings, and false accusations. Then He was given a cross to carry to the Hill of the Skull, where they stripped Him of His clothing and hung Him on a cross for all to see. For all to watch Him die.

After the Passover, the two women named Mary went to attend to Jesus's body, and they found no body. They did, however, find an angel in the tomb who explained to them that Jesus was not there. That Jesus had been resurrected, thus fulfilling the words He had given His disciples. And yet we see from scripture that Mary Magdalene may still not have believed that Jesus was alive. Even though the angel told her so, she still had not fully realized that Jesus was in fact alive.

> Early on the first day of the week, while it was still dark, Mary Magdalene went to the tomb and saw that the stone had been removed from the entrance. So she came running to Simon Peter and the other disciple, the one Jesus loved, and said, "They have taken the Lord out of the tomb, and we don't know where they have put him!"
>
> So Peter and the other disciple started for the tomb. Both were running, but the other disciple outran Peter and reached the tomb first. He bent over and looked in at the strips of linen lying there but did not go in. Then Simon Peter, who was behind him, arrived and went into the tomb. He saw the strips of linen lying there, as well as the burial cloth that had been around Jesus' head. The cloth was folded up by itself, separate from the linen. Finally the other disciple, who had reached the tomb first, also went inside. He saw and believed. (They still did not understand from Scripture that Jesus had to rise from the dead.) (John 20:1–9 NIV)

Resurrection Sunday holds a special meaning for me. It is the time of the year when we celebrate Jesus as He fulfills

His earthly purpose. And Easter is a time of renewal, of rededication. A time of remembering the ways God has come through for me. How He has taken care of me. How He has blessed me. And how He has gently but firmly not fulfilled my prayer requests when they were not things I should have.

This year's Resurrection Easter is different. We all are being told to stay six feet from one another, which means there are no hugs, no handshakes, no human touch. And yet here we are, all types of people who have been brought together with something much stronger than the human touch. Stronger than the invisible monster known as COVID-19.

We are a people who are bound together by something Jesus gave us the moment we accepted Him as our sacrificial Lamb—the Holy Spirit. Joint heirs of the place where God lives known as Heaven. For we are the children of God.

Our love for Jesus Christ sprinkled with this Holy Spirit makes us of one accord, and our love for one another strengthens our bond. Jesus told us that He was our great shepherd and that no one—no person, no virus, nothing—could snatch us from His hands. And that, my Christian friend, is a promise you can count on.

> My sheep listen to my voice; I know them, and they follow me. I give them eternal life, and they shall never perish; no one can snatch them out of my hand. My Father, who has given them to me, is greater than all, no one can snatch them out of my Father's hand. I and the Father are one. (John 10:27–30 NIV)

So, as we celebrate this Resurrection Sunday in a different way, let us remember that

1. Jesus is still with us,
2. He willingly died on the cross as our sacrificial Lamb,
3. He rose from His grave, folded His funeral linens, and walked out of the tomb,
4. He is still our redeemer—the Messiah—the one who gave us the Holy Spirit, and
5. He is the same yesterday, today, and tomorrow.

No virus, no business closings, and no physical separation from fellow believers will ever change these facts.

Chicken Watching

I have six baby chicks. That makes me a chicken farmer. A new chicken farmer at that. Having been told that they died easily from heart attacks, I am slowly introducing my baby chicks to the world. Every day, I set their cage on the grass just a few feet from the only haven they have known, the feed shed. And, oh, how they love it. They seem to really enjoy the warmth of the sun and will instinctively pick at the grass. And yes, I am sitting with them. It gives me writing time.

Off just a short distance away, I hear the call of a hawk. A hungry hawk. A hawk that has just spotted lunch. And so do the chicks. Each time the hawk calls out, the six chicks freeze. They are so still you cannot tell if they are breathing.

And then the chicks do a really cool thing. They freeze in place. And when they freeze, they do so together as if they were one. This enables them to use their natural camouflage in such a way that no one can tell how many chicks are in the cage or how large they are. You cannot tell where they begin and where they end. I have heard that zebras do the same thing. Funny how they instinctively know to do this—freeze in this manner when danger is lurking.

Sometimes, nature just seems to be a bit more obedient to God's ways that the one who was made in His image—man. The moon and sun come and go as God tells them to. Dark clouds form and drop rain on the crops chosen by God. Animals instinctively know how to birth their young.

And how to raise them. Oh, what lessons in obedience we could be taught if we would only watch nature.

The one thing that struck home with me the most, however, was the chicken hawk. The bad man in this story. He announced his coming loudly and clearly before his actual arrival. He seemed to be playing fair by giving the chicks time to hide or flee. While he was on his way down to where the chicks and I were sitting, he was calling out in warning, "Ready or not, here I come!"

We too have a chicken hawk lurking and looking for those he can devour. Looking for his lunch. Satan. He is the bad man in our story. However, unlike the chicken hawk, Satan does not play fair. I have never heard him announce his coming before his actual arrival. Instead, he sneaks up on his prey hoping to overtake them. He tries to trick us. And, if that doesn't work, he tries twisting the Word just ever so slightly. He waits quietly and patiently until we are tired, ill, injured, discouraged, or hindered in some other way, and then he attacks. He moves in for the kill. He tries to destroy us.

Are you surprised? Satan has never been known to play fair. He lies and cheats and does whatever it takes to destroy us. He is known as a murderer and the father of lies. Jesus told us that lying was Satan's native language. And lie he does. Full-fledged lies. Lies of omission. Half-truth lies. And his specialty, the lie of doubts. Jesus, Himself, said:

> "You are of your father the devil, and the
> desires of your father you want to do. He was
> a murderer from the beginning, and does
> not stand in the truth, because there is no
> truth in him. when he speaks a lie, he speaks

from his own resources, for he is a liar and the father of it." (John 8:44 NKJV)

We are also told that Satan roams to and fro looking for someone to devour just as the hawk does.

> Be sober, be vigilant; because your adversary the devil walks about like a roaring lion, seeking whom he may devour. (1 Peter 5:8 NKJV)

Satan loves nothing more than taking down Christians. They are the icing on his cake. The largest notch on his gun belt. His most treasured trophy. A sweet spot in his life. That is why we are told to be sober and watchful.

But all is not lost. If you have accepted Jesus as your Savior, you have been washed in His blood, which is very powerful. It can camouflage you and heal any injuries you suffer at Satan's hands should you ever step out from under its protection.

So, remember, my Christian family—stay sober, vigilant, and stay under the blood of Jesus Christ <u>at all</u> times. Be watchful. Because Satan does not announce he is coming. He just comes.

What I Learned in Bible Study

One day at Bible study, we read in Revelation Chapter 5 about a scroll that has writing on the inside and on the outside and was sealed with seven seals. John wept at the thought that there was no one who was found worthy of looking at the scroll much less opening it. No one in heaven, on the earth or under the earth were worthy of this task.

No one except the Lion of Judah. The Root of David. Jesus Christ, our Savior and sacrificial sin Lamb. He alone is worthy. Jesus took the scroll from the right hand of Him who sits on the throne—God—opened each seal and read the scroll.

> And I looked, and behold, in the midst of the throne and of the four living creatures, and in the midst of the elders, stood a Lamb as though it had been slain, having seven horns and seven eyes, which are the seven Spirits of God sent out into all the earth. Then He came and took the scroll out of the right hand of Him who sat on the throne. Now when He had taken the scroll, the four living creatures and the twenty-four elders fell down before the Lamb, each having a harp, and golden bowls full of incense, which are the prayers of the saints.
>
> And they sang a new song, saying: "You are worthy to take the scroll, and to open its

seals: For You were slain and have redeemed us to God by Your blood out of every tribe and tongue and people and nation, and have made us kings and priests to our God: And we shall reign on the earth." (Revelation 5:6–8 NKJV)

My Bible study teacher rested on the lamb for a few minutes. He explained that in the days of the Old Testament, when blood sacrifices were required, the family was to take a lamb into their homes and tend to it for four days prior to taking its life. I think spending four days with a cute, snuggly, innocent little lamb, feeding it and tending to it daily be it four or forty days, would make the act of sending it to the altar as a sacrifice for my sins extremely hard.

The fact that the lamb had shared my home would make his death as my sacrificial lamb extremely personal. Here is this perfect little lamb, for God required a lamb without blemish, hanging out on my back porch. I feed it and give it water. And the lamb willingly accepts the food and water from me. It has no knowledge that in less than four days, it will lose its life as a sacrifice for the sins of the very one who was tending to him. If the sacrifice of a lamb that had shared my home for four days is so extremely personal to me, how much more personal is the sacrifice of my sacrificial Lamb, Jesus, to His heavenly Father. Jesus, God's only Son, had been with God since the beginning of time. We find in John 1:1–2 that the Word was with God and the Word was God. He became flesh and walked among us. In Scriptures we see Jesus called the glory of the one and only who came from the Father full of glory and grace. Then as if to affirm His identity, Jesus actually told us that He and the Father were one: "I and the Father are one" (John 10:30 NIV).

Jesus is the Son of God and the Lamb of God who has been with God since before the creation of time. God loved us so much that He asked Jesus to lay His life down as our sacrificial Lamb to atone for all our sins forever. Thus, giving us an eternity with Him in heaven.

Thank you, God, for loving us so much, and thank you, Jesus, for your willingness to die for us.

The Mishap—Part 1

One afternoon while riding a horse, I was shown how God could allow us to go through the consequences of our choices, bless us with His mercy, and use us all at the same time. Late one Saturday, I was quickly saddling a horse I had been training. Since darkness was on the way and I wanted to get in some ride time, I stepped it up a bit. As long as I followed all the safety checks, speed was not necessarily a bad thing.

The horse was not fully trained and not trustworthy; she had been misbehaving from the time I had brought her in to saddle her up. My inner voice was telling me to get off the horse and to lunge her, but I wanted to ride. Lunging her meant I would have to get off, take her to the cross ties, and change out my gear. Then instead of riding in the arena, I would have to work from the ground in the round pen.

Yes, she was behaving badly and should had been corrected on a lunge line. But I, being my humble best, said, "I'm a very good rider. I've been riding all my life and should be able to just ride her through her problem." Sound familiar? Like pride maybe? And pride comes before what? A fall maybe?

It was just moments later when everything went downhill fast. The horse started humping in the back, a sign of an upcoming buck. I asked her for a good, strong trot, which usually eliminated any ability of bucking. *Usually* being the key word here.

Instead of obediently striking off in a trot, the horse dropped to her knees on her front legs and popped me off with her strong rear legs. As I soared over the horse's head, I saw the tops of her ears—not a good sign; to see what I was seeing, I must have been standing on my head in midair flying over the horse's head.

Funny how such events seem to happen in their own time. While flying through the air upside down, I thought, *Wow. This is going to hurt.* But to my surprise, my landing was quite soft. Instead of broken bones, I suffered only broken pride and a bruised back. It was almost as if God had shown me mercy and had sent angels to soften my blow.

An eyewitness said that I seemed to be flying in slow motion and landed as if someone had broken my fall. She said that such an accident had broken Christopher Reeve's back. Could I really have been tended to by angels?

If only I had listened to God and had done things His way, not mine, I would not have been thrown. Could the voice that had told me to lunge the horse been the Holy Spirit's warning me of danger?

Though I had disobeyed God, He had mercy on me and sent angels to soften my fall. While He did not take away the consequence of my disobedience—being thrown—He did help me through it. This incident became one of my many testimonies of how God can and does take care of His own. What a wonderful and loving God we serve!

> For He shall give His angels charge over you,
> to keep you in all your ways, in their hands
> they shall bear you up, lest you dash your
> foot against a stone. (Psalm 91:11–12 NKJV)

When the woman who had witnessed my fall realized that she had seen God's hand at work, she was touched.

Unbeknown to me then, she had been in a season of wondering if God was real and wandering from her walk. Seeing God protect me from a potentially extremely life-changing accident softened her heart toward God and allowed her to return to her walk with Him. Wow!

The Mishap—Part 2

However, God was not done with me.

Riders who are thrown must get back on their horses if they can; otherwise, horses will try to throw the next people who ride them. So back on I went. Pushing through the pain that was now pulsing through my lower back, I did what any good rider does—ride out the bucks. After a horrible ride, I finally won the war. I put the horse up and tended to my gear. It was then time to care for myself. I went to the emergency room for X-rays to make sure nothing was broken. While waiting for the results, the ER doctor asked me how long I had been riding and how my accident had occurred. Was I wearing a helmet? How long had it been since I was last thrown? Not remembering the last time, I turned to my husband for an answer, and we concluded that it had been at least ten to fifteen years.

Then the doctor asked me for my advice on a horse he was looking to buy; he was new to horseback riding, and the horse he was looking at was three years old and a beautiful Arab. The sellers assured him that the horse was extremely broke and gentle.

I told him that since he was not experienced with horses, his prospective purchase was not a good match for him. I said that Arabians can be quite a handful for even experienced riders. I asked him just how much training a three-year-old horse could have had considering it had spent its first year at its mother's side. I strongly suggested that he look for an older quarter horse gelding as a first horse, one that was at least ten years old, maybe a retired cow horse or farm horse because they were usually more stable in their behavior and had been alive long enough to be truly trained.

Months later as I was cleaning out a paddock, I saw the most gorgeous quarter horse ridden by a man. What a beautiful picture they made as they seemed to be a perfect fit in size and temperament. The man rode over to me and noticing that I did not recognize him, he introduced himself as the ER doctor who treated me for my riding accident. He thanked me for helping him. He was enjoying riding very much because of the horse he had found, which was gentle and stable. The doctor said that he had learned to trust his horse and felt safe riding him.

So, you see, God used me even in my fallen state *and* even though I had been disobedient. A woman returned to her walk with Jesus, and a man found a good horse for himself. If God can use me, an ordinary person, He can use you too even if you are not always obedient. God is not a respecter of persons.

Ever Say?

Have you ever allowed your emotions to control what you say? You are so angry or hurt that you engage your mouth before your brain and make comments like, "I'm not going to church ever again! Did you see how Sarah treated me? She was so rude! And she calls herself a Christian. I think I'll never talk with anyone else who is from that church ever again!"

Sounds silly, doesn't it? Not going to church again ever just because someone was rude to you. And yet this is exactly what we do in the most important part of our life— the area of our faith in Jesus Christ as our Savior and in God as our heavenly Father. I know I have. How about you?

When the praise team I had been a part of for several years was disbanded, I told God that I did not want to do His music for Him anymore. It was too painful. The tearing away of others who had been such an integral part of my life for years created almost more pain than I could bear. The loss of not only my partners in worship but my prayer partners as well made me feel I was divorcing seven people all at once. Painful!

When a pastoral change in my church caused a great upheaval not just for me but also for others I deeply loved, I told God I never wanted to be that close to another human being again be they Christian or non-Christian. Close relationships were just way too painful.

But I think God found my statements just as silly as the ones listed above. God knew I was filled with unbelievable pain that had prompted my outbursts. In His great mercy, He did not hold me to my words. Looking back, I see that

God was working out my life in accordance with His Word; He had promised His children that He would work out all things for their good. But sometimes, that working out all things for our good can be downright painful. Doing God's work and being in God's will is not always hunky-dory and without discomfort.

But didn't God do the same for me? Did He not worked out things for my salvation when He sent His Son to the cross to die as my sacrificial Lamb? Don't you think that it was painful for God to ask Jesus to take on all our sins?

Moving forward several years, I now see God's promise in Romans 8:28. I sing with a praise team again. I am not only working once again as a church secretary but doing so from the comfort of my home office. Thank you, Lord.

Though there are times when it looks as if God is not working for your good, He is. Just the time that it seems as though He has left you to fend for yourself, He has not. He is working all types of miracles behind the scenes for the good of His children, for the good of those who love Him and are called according to His purpose.

> And we know that in all things God works for the good of those who love him, who have been called according to his purpose. (Romans 8:28 NIV)

And unlike man, God keeps His promises.

Flashlights

Once, I was in a tool store looking for a common household flashlight, but all I could find were flashlights with special features. Some would blink or hang upside down, and some would stick to a metal tool cabinet. I did not see just a plain ol' common household flashlight, you know, like those that ladies use in scary movies when they go outside to see what the noise was.

One flashlight caught my attention. It could be used as a regular flashlight, or the insides could be removed, and its light would radiate like a large candle filling up a room. I used to like being in the dark. No one could see what I was doing. Darkness felt comfortable. Almost soothing. Of course, I would bump into things or fall into pits. But with light, I can see any danger in front of me. I can see where to put my feet as I walk. I can see where I am going as well as where I have been. And with light, others can also see what I do - and where I go.

Isn't that the way it is with our spiritual walk? Before we accepted Jesus Christ as our Savior, we liked being in the dark. When we are in the dark, others cannot see what we are doing or where we are going. But in His light, they can. Jesus's light reflected just how dirty and sinful our lives were.

Before we accepted Jesus Christ as our Savior, we were stumbling around bumping into things and falling into pits. We had nothing to guide our footsteps. We had not accepted God's flashlight, Jesus Christ. Jesus is a beam of light that burns brightly for miles and miles on the darkest of nights. His light fills the rooms of our hearts.

Jesus is the light that shines on us, on our lives, allowing others to see how Christians live. Where they go. What they do. And it allows others to see how God and Jesus care for those who have put their faith and trust in them.

God and His Word along with Jesus are like the flashlight that caught my attention. Sometimes, their light is an intense beam, and sometimes, it is a softer, room-filling light. Either way, it allows us to see where we are going, how to get there, and any danger lurking about.

And oddly enough, it is a light that seems to burn brighter when the times are the darkest. The times when we need it the most.

> When Jesus spoke again to the people, he said, "I am the light of the world. Whoever follows me will never walk in darkness but will have the light of life." (John 8:12 NIV)

My Friend

Our church has suffered a great loss—the passing of one of its pillars. This strong, godly man was a member of the church's board and a close friend of mine. When I went to visit him for the last time, I saw a physical body that had succumbed to an internal enemy called cancer. And his time of passing from this earth to heaven was very near. So near in fact that he may have been talking with the Savior as his body organs were kept alive with a ventilator.

Looking down at what was left of my friend, I remembered what God's Word tells us, that being absent from the body is to be present with the Lord.

> We are confident, yes, well pleased rather to
> be absent from the body and to be present
> with the LORD. (2 Corinthians 5:8 NKJV)

As these words rang through my mind, I saw my friend's cancer-ridden body as just a shell, a shell of a man who had the Holy Spirit living in him. A shell that allowed him to hug me, to go places with me, and to laugh with me. A shell that contained one of the kindest, most gentle souls I had ever known. But a shell, nonetheless.

Since being absent from the body is to be present with the Lord, my friend is now with the Lord. He is not dead as those who do not understand scripture and the things of God believe. He is present with the Lord. He has simply moved from earth to heaven. All of God's children will move from earth to heaven when their time on this earth ends.

God's Word tells us that everyone has an appointed time to die.

> There is a time for everything, and a season
> for every activity under heaven: a time to be
> born and a time to die, a time to plant and
> a time to uproot, (Ecclesiastes 3:1–2 NIV)

We will *all* pass from this earth to somewhere else when our time on this earth ends. It will be a move for eternity, and it will be a move to either heaven or hell. One place or the other. The choice is ours.

Nothing Is Hidden

As I help my friend's family tend to his affairs, I realize once again God's Word is true: any sin, any secret, anything done in darkness will be brought to light. Jesus told us,

> "For there is nothing hidden which will not be revealed, nor has anything been kept secret but that it should come to light." (Mark 4:22 NKJV)

And so, it is when your heirs are tending to your affairs. When you pass from earth to heaven, you will take nothing with you. Whatever you have been reading, eating … the medications you have been taking, the clothes you have been wearing, clean and dirty, your brand of toothpaste, on and on, will be exposed to those who are taking care of your affairs. Any hidden sins, habits, or addictions will no longer be hidden from the light. Jesus knows about them, and so will your family.

The most comforting part of this is that some of my friend's exposures may become his legacies. Traces of his strong faith in Jesus, of his daily Bible reading, his financial support of ministries, and his hidden acts of kindness and mercy are now exposed to his heirs. And maybe he left behind a journal, a written account of how God came through for him. How God helped him be there for his ailing wife. How God listened to and attended to his needs.

What will your heirs find when they are tending to your affairs? What will they uncover? If you were there with them as they rummaged through your things, would you be embarrassed at what they would find? Would your bookshelf or medicine cabinet expose a secret sin? If, your answer is even just a weak "maybe", allow me to remind you that even if your heirs do not know about such things, God does.

> The LORD looks from heaven; He sees all the sons of men. From the place of His dwelling He looks on all the inhabitants of the earth; He fashions their hearts individually; He considers all their works. (Psalm 33:13–15 NKJV)

God knows what we do. He knows what we say, where we go, and with whom we do these things. And He knows things no man could know. He knows our hearts. He knows why we do what we do. He knows if our motives are pure or not. And most important—He knows if we have Jesus in our hearts. Let that sink in. God knows if we have accepted His Son as our Savior. As our sacrificial Lamb. We can run around telling everyone that we are Christians, and some might believe us. But God knows if we are truly Christian. Knows if we are truly followers of His Son. Knows if we are His children. Or not.

We will have to give an account for all our actions. Be they good or bad. Done in secret or openly.

> Nothing in all creation is hidden from God's sight. Everything is uncovered and laid bare before the eyes of him to whom we must give account. (Hebrews 4:13 NIV)

So please, my fellow Christian, remember these scriptures when you want to stray from the path God has laid before you. When you have stopped following Jesus's lead, take a moment and remember that one day, such actions will lie naked before the Lord God, Himself.

And when Satan starts whispering in your ear telling you that you can do it just this once, that no one will know, remember two things. God will know. And Satan is a liar.

Holding On?

Sometimes, it's harder to let go of something and let God take care of it than it is to just continue holding onto it whether it be a trial or just a good ol' case of the what ifs. Sometimes, giving these things to God can feel like giving up.

Giving up is not very popular. Most of us were taught from childhood not to give up. We were told that giving up was not an option. As we grew older, we heard stories about those who were great, important, and successful never giving up. We were taught that no matter what happened, no matter what trial we were undergoing, we were not to give up. We were to persevere through all the murky trials and troubles. In this text, giving up has an extremely negative connotation.

God has told us to persevere in our faith and our walk with Him, but at times, we are to give our trials to God. Times when we are to let Him take care of things. Times when we must allow Him to tend to them in the way He sees best. And to do so in His time, not ours. Giving these times totally to God can be quite difficult. And even more so for those who are accustomed to doing.

And then there is the trust side of giving our trials to God. Will He take care of it? We know He can, but will He?

I have had these types of thoughts, haven't you? We tend to base our relationship with God on the relational experiences that we have had with other people. We have no other references for relationships. However, this people-relationship reference is very poor. People will always let us down at some time in our relationships with them. They will at times use us, not treat us well, and say mean things to us. They will not always be thoughtful, and they maybe will even beat us up some. For they are people, and people do people things. Even Christians do people things.

Because of this, we can find it extremely hard to trust that God is not the same. It can be hard for us to grasp how much God loves us and how consistent he in His relationship with us. It is hard for us to trust God to take care of all our trials and our what ifs. So, we tend to hold onto them.

There is also the issue of the loss of control when we turn our trials and what ifs over to God; when we have done so, God then has control over them, which can cause us to feel vulnerable. And in this world of uncertainty, where there appears to be a loss of control over such things as the economy, health care, and freedom of speech, losing control over just one more thing makes us very uncomfortable almost to the point of being unbearable.

But God always has control over all things, always. Even though we may think we have control over things, we do not. God does. We do, however, have control over our actions and our decision to release our control over our trials and what ifs. To allow God to take care of them. To allow God to be in control. To allow God to be God.

God is a great and merciful God and a real gentleman. If you tell Him that you want to take care of your trials and your what ifs by yourself, He will stand back and let you try. He will not take from you whatever you aren't willing to give to Him.

Are you strong enough to release your trials and your what ifs to God? Are you willing to give Him control over your trials? Will you trust Him with your what ifs? Or are you still holding onto them? Do you have to keep control at any cost? Ultimately, it all comes down to trust. Do you trust God? Do you have faith in Him and in His love for you?

God has promised that He will not let the righteous, His children, fall.

> Cast your cares on the LORD and he will
> sustain you; he will never let the righteous
> fall. (Psalm 55:22 NIV)

And God keeps His promises.

If You Need It—Give It Away

God told us to be generous. He told us that we would receive if we gave and, the more we give the more we would receive.

In the words of our Savior, Jesus Christ,

> "Give and it will be given to you. A good measure, pressed down, shaken together, and running over, will be poured into your lap. For with the measure you use, it will be measured to you." (Luke 6:38 NIV)

In fact, God had a lot to say about giving. He told us that He would bless us when we generously gave to the poor.

> A generous man will himself be blessed, for he shares his food with the poor. (Proverbs 22:9 NIV)

God loves to see us giving cheerfully. Willingly.

> Remember this: whoever sows sparingly will also reap sparingly, and whoever sows generously will also reap generously. Each man should give what he has decided in his heart to give, not reluctantly or under compulsion, for God loves a cheerful giver. (2 Corinthians 9:6–7 NIV)

These are just some of the many verses found in God's Word instructing us to give generously to others. But could being generous tie in with trusting God? Could the lack of our generosity be more than just a lack of things to give? Could it be a sign of a something else? Let's look at it.

Perhaps our lack of generosity is fear based due to our own lack. Perhaps there are times we are afraid to be generous with others because of our own needs. We have so little, and what we do have, we need.

But scriptures tell us otherwise. We are told that in fact, should we share with others, God will supply us with not only what we need but with extra so we can share again.

> Now he who supplies seed to the sower and bread for food will also supply and increase your store of seed and will enlarge the harvest of your righteousness. You will be made rich in every way so that you can be generous on every occasion, and through us your generosity will result in thanksgiving to God. (2 Corinthians 9:10–11 NIV)

Wow! God was telling us that the more we shared, the more we would have to share.

Allow me to share a challenge. For the next thirty days, let us apply this scripture.

1. Need more time? Spend some time with someone who needs you.
2. Need more clothes? Clean out those closets and give away clothes you do not wear any more. Preferably ones without stains and holes. Remember, you will receive in the same manner you give.

3. Need food? Share what food you have with someone in need of food. I once saw a woman going from food pantry to food pantry. While waiting in line, she was sharing what she had with others.
4. Need comfort? Comfort someone who is going through some type of trial or loss.
5. Lonely? Visit someone who lives alone.

This chapter would not be complete without a mention of that infamous thing called money. Do you seem to have more bills than money at the end of the month? You seem to always have an unexpected bill just when you thought you would have some extra money. I have had times like that, but I have learned that when I am faithful in my tithing, God is faithful in His providing. Yes, I may not have a lot of extra money, and what I do have can be eaten up unexpectedly, but have you ever stopped to think that maybe that extra money was God's way of supplying for the upcoming unexpected expenditure?

Maybe you should try tithing even if it's only for the next thirty days. Give God a try. See what He will do. God promised that if you honored Him with your firstfruits, He would fill you barns to overflowing. Not just full - but overflowing full!

> "Bring the whole tithe into the storehouse, that there may be food in my house. Test me in this," says the LORD Almighty, "and see if I will not throw open the floodgates of heaven and pour out so much blessing that you will not have room enough for it. I will prevent pests from devouring your crops, and the vines in your fields will not cast their

fruit," says the LORD Almighty. Then all the
nations will call you blessed, for yours will be
a delightful land," says the LORD Almighty.
(Malachi 3:10–12 NIV)

God has promised to take care of your needs. And
what God has promised, God will do. Sometimes, God
uses people to help take care of your needs. So, could it
be that when you are giving away your clothes, or feeding
someone who is hungry, or even tithing, God is using you?
That He is taking the things you are willingly giving away
and caring for one who has a need for that item? Perhaps
a brother of sister in Christ?

Promises

Proverbs is a book known for its wisdom, but I see God's promises all over it and especially in chapter 3.

Have you ever made a promise to someone? Did you keep that promise no matter the cost? When we make promises, we have all intentions of keeping them, but then circumstances may arise that don't allow us to follow through. You make a promise to pick someone up for lunch, but that morning, you wake up sick and can't make it. Ever happen to you? A well-intended promise turns into a well-intended broken promise. You didn't plan on becoming ill, but you did, and that kept you from keeping your promise.

That is not how it goes with God's promises. When God makes a promise, He keeps it. God does what He promises to do. God's promises are done deals. You can count on them no matter the circumstances.

So, all the promises found in Proverbs, Jeremiah, or anywhere else in God's Word are promises you can count on. What God says He will do, He will do. Whatever God says will happen - will happen. Case closed.

Did God Create Evil?

There was a program on TV debating whether God created evil. One side took the stance that since God created everything and since there is evil in this world, God must have created evil.

Doesn't the question "Did God create evil?" have a familiar ring to it? Yes? I think so too. This question of whether God created evil seems to be nothing more than another one of Satan's wiles. Satan is up to his tried-and-true trick called "just a hint of doubt".

Of course, we all know that evil comes from Satan, the fallen angel. But still, I pondered this question about God's sovereignty. On how Satan was cast from heaven when he wanted God's job, and how Satan was able to take a third of God's angels with him. How these angels were following the lead of Satan and not of God, willingly.

In Genesis, we see how God created the heavens and the earth, day and night, the sky, seas and dry land, plants and trees, the sun and the moon, fish and birds and other animals—everything. When God saw all that He had created, He called it good. No bad or so-so but good. No evil here.

Then God created one more time. He created man. And Jesus was right there with Him. For these verses state let "us" make.

> Then God said, "Let us make man in our image, in our likeness, and let them rule over the fish of the sea and the birds of the air, over the livestock, over all the earth, and over all the creatures that move along the ground."

> So God created man in his own image, in the
> image of God he created him; male and female
> he created them. (Genesis 1:26–27 NIV)

From what I see, God created only good things. Not bad things. Or evil things. But there is evil in this world. Bad things do happen to us and to others. So just where does evil come from? Well, if it is not from God, then it has to be from Satan. For we have only one or the other. God or Satan. No third choice.

But can Satan truly harm those who belong to God?

Remember what happened in the Garden of Eden? Remember how Satan caused Adam and Eve to sin? How he was able to create just enough doubt about God's motive that she did the one and only thing she was not to do? Eat the forbidden fruit?

> "You will not surely die," the serpent said to
> the woman, "For God knows that when you
> eat of it your eyes will be opened, and you
> will be like God, knowing good and evil."

> When the woman saw that the fruit of the
> tree was good for food and pleasing to the
> eye, and also desirable for gaining wisdom,
> she took some and ate it. She also gave some
> to her husband, who was with her, and he ate
> it. (Genesis 3:4–6 NIV)

The very moment she held the forbidden fruit to her lips, Eve had fallen victim to Satan's tried-and-true trick called "just a hint of doubt". Sin was born. And evil entered into our world. Forever.

Why Water?

Jesus told us that He gives Living Water to those who ask for it, and that whoever drinks of His Living Water will never thirst again.

> When a Samaritan woman came to draw water, Jesus said to her, "Will you give me a drink?" (His disciples had gone into the town to buy food.)
>
> The Samaritan woman said to him, "You are a Jew, and I am a Samaritan woman. How can you ask me for a drink?" (For Jews do not associate with Samaritans.)
>
> Jesus answered her, "If you knew the gift of God and who it is that asks you for a drink, you would have asked him and he would have given you living water."
>
> "Sir," the woman said, "you have nothing to draw with and the well is deep. Where can you get this living water? Are you greater than our father Jacob, who gave us the well and drank from it himself, as did also his sons and his flocks and herds?"
>
> Jesus answered, "Everyone who drinks this water will be thirsty again, but whoever drinks the water I give him will never thirst.

Indeed, the water I give him will become in him a spring of water welling up to eternal life." (John 4:7–14 NIV)

Ever wonder why Jesus offers us Living Water? Why He did not offer us living bread. Or living tea? Or maybe even living cake? But Living Water?

Perhaps Jesus gives us Living Water because water is essential for life. Unless we have the proper amount of water, our bodies cannot function. Nor would there be the proper removal of waste and cleansing of tissue. We would develop high blood pressure. Our kidneys would not work. The delicate balance of electrolytes would be interrupted. We could experience dehydration. And each of these situations can be life threatening.

Nature also relies on water. There are far more plants in tropical climates where water is plentiful than in arid climates such as deserts. Have you ever taken a plant that is almost dead and watch its response to proper watering? It comes back to life and grows. For without water, it would not survive.

Water cleans and refreshes. Walk outside after a thunderstorm and take in a great big breath. What a treat. Smell that wonderfully clean air. Feel how it seems to incite a feeling of wellness. Of peace. Of serenity. Of being refreshed.

There is also one more feat that water can do. It creates. Yes. Should water drip in the same spot long enough, it creates an imprint that could grow into a river. And water does not care what the spot is made of; the results are the same.

Let us look at the Living Water that Jesus talked about.

Living Water that sustains us. That cleanses us of our sins. Renews us when we are dying plants. Refreshes us. Living Water that created a new creation when we took our first sip.

We need this Living Water to keep from becoming spiritually dehydrated and to keep us filled with God's Holy Spirit. Our souls depend on it. Just like the barren deserts, we will become spiritually barren without the Living Water. There will be no spiritual growth. We cannot produce lots of good spiritual fruit that we can share with others unless we drink of the Living Water Jesus offers us - daily.

And then there is the cleansing. Life is dirty. And we all are in need of a good scrubbing. Some daily, some hourly, and some like me—minute by minute. We need Jesus's Living Water to scrub us up. To cleanse us. To wash away our sins. Our transgressions. Our unrighteousness.

We find that Jesus's Living Water will refresh us. It will give us that *Ahhh!* moment. You know, that *Ahhh!* feeling you get when you jump into a cool pool on a hot day or when you sit down with a glass of cool water after working in the yard.

We also rely on Jesus's Living Water to soothe our thirst when we are journeying through one of life's deserts. When we are having to walk mile after mile in the heat of life's trials. Living Water soothes our souls, refreshes our spirits, and gives us the strength to take another step.

The water we drink and use costs us in some way, but Jesus offers us His Living Water for free. It's there just for the taking. And we can have as much as we want as often as we want and at any time we want it. All we have to do is to drink it. Thank you, Jesus!

There Is a New Pastor in Town

For the past nine years, I have had the privilege of being mentored by a very strong and mature pastor, a man of God who taught his flock how to live Christian lives more by how he lived than by what he said. His experience in administration gave him unusual insight into people's strengths, which the Lord used greatly. Not only could this man see the individual needs of each one of his flock, but he could deliver a sermon that would blow your socks off. A sermon that made you feel as if he had been spying on your private life. The Lord has blessed this pastor with the gift of teaching and administration.

But as God's Word teaches us, there is a season for all things. And the season of preaching and teaching for this pastor is now ending, for he is retiring as a pastor. I am not sure that pastors can truly retire; once you're a pastor, you'll always be a pastor. Kind of like being a wife or a parent.

So, our church voted in a younger man, someone in his thirties, to be our new pastor. This man also has a firm grasp of God's Word and a passion for people, and he lives a good, clean, Christian life. But he is different from our previous pastor. The deliverance of his sermons is different. His approach to the business side of the church is different. He looks different. Sounds different.

However, the Lord has shown me something about our new and younger pastor. His heart. He has a deep yearning to see all people saved. All people. Big people. Little people. Old people. Young people. His desire is that no one lives separated from God for eternity. None. Sound familiar?

> For God so loved the world that he gave his
> one and only Son, that whoever believes in
> him shall not perish but have eternal life.
> For God did not send his Son into the world
> to condemn the world, but to save the world
> through him. (John 3:16–17 NIV)

I often wonder what Jesus's disciples thought about Him. He was different. His words were different. The deliverance of His sermons was different. So were His ways. His teachings. Jesus often referred to God as His heavenly Father. In fact, He actually said that He and the heavenly Father were one.

> I and the Father are one. (John 10:30 NIV)

Sure, Jesus's disciples and others had watched Him calm stormy waters, cast out demons, and bring the dead back to life, but they did not have the scriptures to help them fully understand who Jesus was. They did not have God's written Word to sustain them and to help them grasp the idea that Jesus was God's Son. They could not look up John 3:16–17 and read that God so loved the world that He sent His one and only Son to save the world. Nor could they turn to Matthew 3 and read how the second Jesus was baptized God proclaimed that Jesus was His Son in whom He was well pleased.

> As soon as Jesus was baptized, he went up
> out of the water. At that moment heaven
> was opened, and he saw the Spirit of God
> descending like a dove and lighting on
> him. And a voice from heaven said, "This

is my Son, whom I love; with him I am well
pleased." (Matthew 3:16–17 NIV)

And yet, they were drawn to Jesus. They learned from
Jesus, and they followed Him.

And so, it is with our new, young pastor. The Lord
allowed me a glimpse of his heart, and I saw the softness
of Jesus radiating from him. I saw that same love for others
Jesus had. I saw a great strength being checked by humility.
I saw that even though he was different from our retired
pastor, he was just as good. Just as sincere. Just as loving.

Our church had enjoyed the leadership of our retired
pastor for many years, but that season ended, and we have
entered a new one. I thank my Lord for my old pastor, who
matured me spiritually, and for my new pastor, who will
now help me see my Christian walk in a new way.

The Parallel of Adam and Abraham

Adam's sin caused circumstances that the world has had to live with ever since it was committed. The sin and death that it brought into the world has been handed down from generation to generation.

> Therefore, just as sin entered the world through one man, and death through sin, and in this way death came to all men, because all sinned- (Romans 5:12 NIV)

Satan told Eve just enough of the truth mixed with lies that she fell for his wiles -hook, line, and sinker. He created just a touch of doubt about God's motive behind His commandment. So, Eve doubted, ate of the fruit and sinned. And because of this, women suffer during childbirth.

> To the woman he said, "I will greatly increase your pains in childbearing; with pain you will give birth to children. Your desire will be for your husband, and he will rule over you." (Genesis 3:16 NIV)

However, Adam was there with Eve. And even though God had told him directly not to eat of this fruit, Adam took the fruit from his wife's hand and ate. In fact, should truth be known, God told Adam not to eat from the tree of knowledge of good and evil before Eve was even there. Before she was created.

But God is a just and fair God. Eve was not the only one who was given negative circumstances for sin, Adam was too. Because Adam was there at the scene with Eve, and participated in the same sin, we must now toil for our food. We must now endure such things as weeds and thorns. And for those of us in Florida - sandspurs. Ouch!

> To Adam he said, "Because you listened to your wife and ate from the tree about which I commanded you, 'You must not eat of it,' cursed is the ground because of you; through painful toil you will eat of it all the days of your life. It will produce thorns and thistles for you, and you will eat the plants of the field. By the sweat of your brow you will eat your food until you return to the ground, since from it you were taken; for dust you are and to dust you will return."
> (Genesis 3:17–19 NIV)

And then there is Abraham.

Abraham's sin of not waiting on God for the chosen son caused him to lay with Hagar as if she were his wife. And the seed from that union produced Ishmael. A wild man. A hostile man whose hand is against every man with every man's hand against him. A father of many descendants. A man believed to be the beginning of the Arab nation.

Once again, the world is to live with the circumstances of one man's actions from that time forward. Only this time it was Abraham's.

> The angel of the LORD found Hagar near a spring in the desert; it was the spring that is

beside the road to Shur. And he said, "Hagar, servant of Sarai, where have you come from, and where are you going?"

"I'm running away from my mistress Sarai," she answered.

Then the angel of the LORD told her, "Go back to your mistress and submit to her." The angel added, "I will so increase your descendants that they will be too numerous to count."

The angel of the LORD also said to her: "You are now with child and you will have a son. You shall name him Ishmael, for the LORD has heard of your misery. He will be a wild donkey of a man; his hand will be against everyone and everyone's hand against him, and he will live in hostility toward all his brothers." (Genesis 16:7–12 NIV)

In both these stories, we see a parallel; the actions of these two men affected not only themselves but all others, not just those who believe in Jesus or those who live in a certain nation but all people of all generations. People will have to live with the results of the actions of these two men and a woman until Jesus returns.

The circumstances of sin:

Adam's sin—hard work and sandspurs.
Eve's sin—labor pains.

Abraham' sin—the birthing of a hostile nation.

So, the next time you think that your sins, be they done openly or in secret, will not harm anyone, think again. No sin affects only us. Sin, yours and mine, will always cause problems for others and may do so for a very long time. There are always negative circumstances attached to sin, no matter whose sin it is.

And it just may be that those who are being adversely affected by this sin are innocent bystanders.

Sin Is *Messy*

> When he reached home, he took a knife and cut up his concubine, limb by limb, into twelve parts and sent them into all the areas of Israel. (Judges 19:29 NIV)

Wow! When I first read this verse, I cringed. How gruesomely graphic. How could a man cut up a woman who had not only saved him from being raped by other men, but was a woman with whom he had been intimate?

This verse was taken from Judges 19, a story about a Levite who went to get his concubine after she ran back to her father's home. The concubine's father had convinced the Levite to stay for four nights. But on the fifth day, the Levite insisted on leaving the father's camp even though it was becoming late. The Levite along with his concubine had to put up somewhere for the night and tried to find a place in the city of Gibeah in Benjamin, but no one offered them a place to stay.

As the men were coming in from the fields, an old man saw the Levite and his concubine in the town square. He noticed they were travelers and asked them where they were going. The Levite explained that they had been to Bethlehem and were on their way to a remote area in the hill country of Ephraim.

The old man asked the two to stay with him for the night stating that it was not safe for them to spend the night in the town square, so they went to the old man's home. Once the old man tended to the Levite's donkeys, he washed the feet of his guest, fed them supper, and provided them with something to drink.

As the three were enjoying each other's company, some wicked men of the town surrounded the old man's home. They pounded on the door and demanded that the old man throw the Levite out into the streets, for they wanted to have sexual relations with him.

Instead of giving into the demands of these wicked men, the old man stepped outside and asked them not to do such vile and wicked things to his guest. He offered his virgin daughter and the Levite's concubine instead.

So, the wicked men took the Levite's concubine and raped and abused her all night. Once the sun rose, the concubine was able to get back to the old man's house, but she collapsed and died at his doorstep. When the Levite man found her, he placed her on his donkey and took her home. He then cut her body up into twelve pieces and sent them to his neighbors. Imagine being his neighbor and having him deliver to you something wrapped up and bloody. Shocking to say the least. Why would something this horrible and graphic be in God's Word?

But wait a moment. Is this not what God sees when He sees our sin? Is not our sin just as horrible and graphic as the actions of the Levite? Isn't our sin just as gruesome? And have we not sent pieces of our sin to our neighbors for them to see? Or maybe even to participate in?

Yes, this scripture is very distasteful. And yes, it makes our insides cringe. But so, it is with God. He finds our unrepented sin—sin that has not been placed under the blood of Jesus—just as distasteful. Just as gruesome. And yes, this scripture is bloody. But so is sin. Yours. Mine. All sin.

Sin requires a blood offering for atonement. Sin requires the blood of the sacrificial sin Lamb—Jesus Christ.

> This is my blood of the covenant, which is poured out for many for the forgiveness of sins. (Matthew 26:28 NIV)

I Hear Sorrow in God's Voice

Hear, O heavens! Listen, O earth! For the LORD has spoken:

> "I reared children and brought them up, but they have rebelled against me. The ox knows his master, the donkey his owner's manger, but Israel does not know, my people do not understand."

> "Ah, sinful nation, a people loaded with guilt, a brood of evildoers, children given to corruption! They have forsaken the LORD; they have spurned the Holy One of Israel and turn their backs on him."

> "Why should you be beaten anymore? Why do you persist in rebellion? You whole head is injured, your whole heart afflicted. From the sole of your foot to the top or your heard there is no soundness – only wounds and welts and open sores, not cleansed or bandaged or soothed with oil."

> "Your country is desolate, your cities burned with fire; your fields are being striped by foreigners right before you, laid waste as when overthrown by strangers." (Isaiah 1:2–7 NIV)

"Come now, let us reason together," says the Lord. "Though your sins are like scarlet, they shall be as white as snow; though they are red as crimson, they shall be like wool. If you are willing and obedient, you will eat the best from the land; but if you resist and rebel, you will be devoured by the sword." For the mouth of the LORD has spoken. (Isaiah 1:18–20 NIV)

Hear the sorrow in God's voice as He speaks about His children. Hear God's concern for them. How much He cares for them. He talks about His children having open wounds and welts from their heads to their feet. Open wounds that have not been cleansed. And welts that have not been treated with oil.

God's children have turned away from Him. They are rebelling against Him. And yet, God asks them to come to Him. To talk with Him. For even though they are doing such things, He still desires a relationship with them. Wow!

The very God who created all things. Who gave us our sacrificial Lamb? Who caused rocks to give water, and ravens to feed men, is asking His children to come to Him? Not demanding. Asking. God longs to talk with us about things. He yearns to heal our sickness. Cleanse our wounds. Relieve our pains and hurts.

There have been times when we have been children filled with evil and rebellion. All of us. Everyone. Even those who were brought up in church. We all have lives prior to accepting Jesus as our personal Savior. And yet He asks us to come to Him so that He may talk with us, be with us, tend to us, provide for us, and protect us. Though we have been far less that good children, God still desires to have a relationship with us. He still wants to be our heavenly Father; and He still wants us to be His children.

Too Familiar?

As I watched my thirty-year-old nephew being ordained as a pastor, I remembered when he was a young boy swimming in the canal with his sister. The times when his dad would gently talk to him about his behavior. When he would try to get out of doing what he was supposed to do. Or that little boy trying to sneak a cookie from the cookie jar. That seemed like only yesterday, but there he was, the spiritual leader of a church.

Isn't that just like family? You can be the most famous person and yet your family views you as just plain ol' John or plain ol' Sarah. Jesus had to deal with this as well. He was traveling around doing all types of miracles, healings, and casting out of demons. In between His miracle, He was teaching anyone who would listen to Him.

He had become well know with the Pharisees. And yet when He returned to His hometown, they would not accept Him as the Messiah, as the Savior God had sent them.

Instead, they viewed Him as the carpenter's son. As Mary's son. As the brother to James, Judas, and Simon. Or as the older brother to His sisters. They did not refer to Jesus as their Messiah. Or as the one and only Son of God. Or as their Savior, Or even as their teacher. They even took offense with Him. As Jesus, along with His disciples, was at the synagogue teaching, the people of his hometown were saying things such as, "How can Jesus think He is the Messiah?" "He's Joseph's son. He and my boys played together when they were young." "Is He really doing miracles?" "My wife and I used to watch over Jesus for Joseph and Mary." "We watched Him grow up. And now He comes back home and teaches in the synagogue?"

> Jesus left there and went to his hometown, accompanied by his disciples. When the Sabbath came, he began to teach in the synagogue, and many who heard him were amazed.

> "Where did this man get these things?" they asked. "What's this wisdom that he has been given him, that he even does miracles! Isn't this the carpenter? Isn't this Mary's son and the brother of James, Joseph's Judas and Simon? Aren't his sisters here with us?" And they took offense at him. (Mark 6:1–3 NIV)

Because Jesus was too familiar to His earthly family and because His earthly family was too familiar with those who lived in His hometown, it was extremely hard for them to believe that Jesus could really be the Son of God. And even harder for them to believe that He could in fact be the Messiah. Had they not seen Him grow up there with their children?

Sadly, their lack of faith in Jesus—in what He was telling them—in who He was - removed His ability to do miracles for the very people He may have grown up with.

> Jesus said to them, "Only in his hometown, among his relatives and in his own house

is a prophet without honor." He could not do any miracles there, except lay his hands on a few sick people and heal them. And he was amazed at their lack of faith. (Mark 6:4–6 NIV)

Housekeeping

As I was sweeping floors, washing dishes, and changing sheets, I was thinking of how much my husband loves a clean house. Cleaning house is a lot of work and requires a lot of equipment such as different soaps, floor cleaners, furniture polish, and so on. And of course, lots of elbow grease.

But the thoughts of how nice a clean house will look and how pleased my husband will be make me work even harder. I love my husband, and I like to see him happy. He works very hard to provide me with this home, and I want to show him honor by keeping it as clean as I can. So, I scrub and scrub, and clean and clean. And I do so with joy.

Housekeeping is an ongoing task with never an end... It seems that dust bunnies and dog hair are just watching and waiting for the very minute I clean the table and then *Boom!* They pounce. Right onto that just-cleaned table. *Arggh!*

Then there's laundry. I gather all the clothes according to their colors and put them in the washer and then into the dryer. Putting up the clean towels in the bathroom, I see it. A piece of dirty clothing hiding behind the dirty laundry basket. *Arggh* again!

Good housekeeping requires daily attention; it's easier to dust every two or three days than it is to drag everything out to the backyard for a good scrubbing every two or three months. Same with the dishes. And with taking out the garbage.

While I was cleaning and scrubbing and scrubbing and cleaning, I realized that our spiritual lives require housekeeping too. Imagine just how please God is when we, His children, live clean lives.

Then there is Jesus, my Bridegroom. He gave His all to provide me with the life I have. And just like my earthly husband, who loves a clean physical house, Jesus loves a clean spiritual house. Keeping my spiritual house clean is a way of worshipping and honoring Him.

Just like housecleaning, spiritual cleaning takes a lot of time and effort. And just as it is with physical housekeeping, spiritual housekeeping is much easier when done daily. It is much easier to deal with those dust bunnies—also known as sin —in the spiritual world if they are dealt with daily. And just like dust bunnies, sin bunnies are just waiting to pounce into a clean heart and dirty it up. The very moment you have allowed Jesus to clean out your heart, your soul, and your mind, here they come—sin bunnies running back with a vengeance looking to pounce back into their old familiar place – you heart. Again, I say - *Arggh!*

We must constantly work at keeping ourselves clean and pure. We must follow the good housekeeping rules found in our Bibles and allow the Holy Spirit to clean our spirits every day. Or even every moment if that's what it takes.

However, unlike housecleaning, our spiritual cleaning tools are straightforward—our Bibles and a desire to follow Jesus is all we need. God has given us the strongest cleanser ever found, the blood of Jesus Christ.

Our loving Lord gave us someone who will help us with our daily spiritual cleaning—the Holy Spirit. And a cleaning manual—the Bible.

Yes, just like housecleaning, spiritual cleaning is hard work, and it never ends. But picture this. You pass from the earth into heaven with a pure and clean spirit and you see Jesus standing there smiling and extending His hand to you as He welcomes you. Imagine how sweet His voice will sound when He tells you well done faithful servant.

Like Wow! Or what!

Therefore, having these promises, beloved, let us cleanse ourselves from all filthiness of the flesh and spirit, perfecting holiness in the fear of God. (2 Corinthians 7:1 NKJV)

Ouch!

My pastor spoke from the book of Titus last week. And for the most part, it was good. That is until I read Chapter 3:1–3. Then God's Word stomped all over my toes. Ouch!

Sometimes, God's Word can be quite prickly. And I was pricked by the Scripture found in Titus 3:1–3.

> Remind them to be subject to rulers and authorities, to obey, to be ready for every good work, to speak evil of no one, to be peaceable, gentle, showing all humility to all men. For we ourselves were also once foolish, disobedient, deceived, serving various lusts and pleasures, living in malice and envy, hateful and hating one another. (Titus 3:1–3 NKJV)

My Bible tells me to be subject to all rulers and authorities bar none. To those with whom I agree and those with whom I do not. Those who I feel do not necessarily favor Christians and the Christian way of life and those who I feel are very much for Christians and the Christian way of life.

Wow. What a large responsibility God has given me. Submitting to a ruler or an authority with whom I disagree. Providing the ruler is not asking me to break one of God's commandments or one of man's laws, I am to do as asked, to submit. And I am asked to so while showing humility. Why would my heavenly Father ask such a thing from me?

How I treat those I am opposed to is my testimony of what walking with Jesus is. Submitting to a ruler who is not portraying the fruits of walking close to Jesus may be an extremely effective testimony of what a Christ follower is like. Perhaps by quietly submitting, I may stand out in the crowd as being different. There are far too many Christians who talk Christianese but walk a worldly walk. Who are not walking their talk?

Sadly enough, during the past few months, I have been one of those Christianese Christians. For I have been extremely verbal about my dislikes and distrust of certain branches of government. Granted, as secretary for my church, I was privy to some insight others did not have access to, but according to this scripture, that doesn't matter; that is no excuse. God's Word tells me to be subject to all authority in spite my inside intel.

And then as if submitting were not enough, Titus 3:1–3 tells me I am to be obedient, yes, obedient to rulers and to those who are in authority. I am to be ready to help all men and do so peaceably with consideration for all my rulers and for all those who are in authority. For all. Period.

Titus 3:1–3 does not tell me to be obedient, ready to help, peaceable, and considerate only when governmental authorities are doing what I think is right, or fair, or good for my country. It says to be gentle and kind, obedient and respectful at all times. Even if those who are authority are stepping on my Christian toes. Even then.

If you read on down in this scripture, you will find that God told us that we too were once foolish, disobedient, envious, and hateful and living just to please ourselves and our desires. For there was a time before accepting Jesus as our personal Savior that we also made the same types of decisions. A time when our spiritual eyes were not open.

A time when maybe we could not know and understand the things of God.

But our spiritual eyes are open. We know and understand the things of God because we belong to Him. And God tells us to treat others gently. We are to be ready to say something nice to them. We are to be at peace with them. For when we do such things, our obedience to God becomes our loudest sermon ever. We will be portraying the very heart of God and of His Son, our Savior, Jesus Christ.

Salt of the Earth

Words from our Lord and Savior, Jesus Christ:

> "You are the salt of the earth; but if the salt loses its flavor, how shall it be seasoned? It is then good for nothing but to be thrown out and trampled underfoot by men." (Matthew 5:13 NKJV)

Why are we to be the salt of the earth? Why not the sugar of the earth? Sugar is sweet and is liked by everyone. This is not always true with salt.

Unlike sugar, salt is a necessary mineral that our bodies need to function. Without the proper amount of salt, our blood pressure among other things would be way out of whack.

But salt does so much more.

Salt creates thirst. We Christians should be creating a thirst for Jesus in others. We should be standing out among the crowd in such a positive way that it causes others to want what we have—a longing for the thirst-quenching Living Water given by Jesus.

Salt preserves. As we go from trial to trial and mission to mission, we should be reflecting how God protects and preserves His children.

Salt flavors. We are to live lives that are filled with the flavor that comes only from God. The flavor is His Son, Jesus. We are to live as fully as we can filled with the blessings God has given us and the work as well.

Salt tenderizes. We Christians are to live with tenderness toward others. We are to treat them with love and respect. For in doing so, we reflect the love Jesus showed us at the cross and the love the God has for us.

Salt heals. When you have a sore in your mouth, you use saltwater to heal it. When you have a sore in your spirit, Jesus heals it. And sometimes He uses people to do that.

Salt cleanses. When you are to clean a wound, doctors now tell you to use normal saline instead of soap. Normal saline is a fancy word for saltwater. When you are in need of a soul cleansing, you have the best cleanser available— the blood of Jesus Christ.

Salt is necessary. Without the proper amount of salt, you can suffer from low blood pressure, which could lead to seizures and even death. And just like salt is crucial to your good physical health, Jesus is crucial for your good spiritual health.

Salt stings. There are times when God's Word can sting. If we are doing or maybe not doing what God has told us to do, His Word can be painful. And it may stay that way until we are obedient.

Because we are salt, not sugar, we thirst for God's ways. We drink from the Living Water. We have protection. We are happier. We can truly love others. We have tender hearts. We have healing. We are cleansed of our sins. We have salvation. We have direction.

The second part of this scripture states that should Christians lose their saltiness, they are good for nothing but being trampled on by men and being thrown out. If we lose our saltiness, we are good for nothing. Strong words. What a great example of God's Word stinging!

There is a reason for these strong words. Christians who lose their saltiness no longer appear to be different.

They look and smell just like everyone else who lives in worldly ways. They blend in because they have lost their saltiness. Unless they stand out from the rest of the crowd, no one will notice them or see that they are different.

People should be able to see Jesus through the life of a Christian. Their words and actions are to reflect Jesus and His ways. This will cause them to appear different from others. This difference, or saltiness, attracts others to the Christians may lead them to Jesus.

However, without this salty attraction, no one will desire to drink of the water that Christians have drink from. For no one would thirst for it. And without this desire for the Living Water, without the thirst created by a salty Christian, they may never accept Jesus as their Savior. They would be doomed to live a life that is filled with unforgiven sin ending with an eternity spent in hell – separated from God. How sad!

Opposites

Christmas … the most wonderful time of the year! The time when we celebrate our Savior's birth. There are Christmas lights and Christmas trees everywhere. People are out buying for others, doing for others. For once, people are thinking of others.

While listening to another sermon on the birth of my Savior, I thought about how Jesus was born. About His life. About His name. And even a little about His appearance. About how different Jesus was. How His name was so powerful that Satan and his demons trembled at the very mention of it.

From what I have read, the name Jesus was relatively common in that time. He was born quietly in a manger that was meant for livestock, not for human birthing. His early years of life were quiet first in Bethlehem and then in Egypt.

We have been told very little about Jesus's physical appearance, but what we do know is that His appearance was ordinary, not anything that would have made Him stand out in a crowd. We often have a mental picture of Jesus appearing tall, strong, and very manly. But according to God's Word, He was ordinary.

> Who has believed our report? And to whom has the arm of the LORD been revealed? For He shall grow up before Him as a tender plant, and as a root out of dry ground, He has no form or comeliness; and when we

see Him, there is no beauty that we should
desire Him. (Isaiah 53:1–2 NKJV)

Jesus quietly walked among us for decades. When He
was confronted by the Jews who wanted to stone Him
because He had proclaimed that He was God's Son, He
spoke to them and then quietly slipped away.

When an army of soldiers accompanied the officers of
church leaders to the garden to arrest Him, Jesus quietly
accepted their arrest. He even reprimanded Peter when he
attempted to protect Him.

Then Jesus quietly stood before a made-up trial in
which facts were either twisted or were outright lies. A trial
where the witnesses were false witnesses. A trial where the
made-up stories given by the so-called witnesses actually
conflicted with each other.

Even though Jesus was flogged almost to the point of
death, was spat on and tormented, He did not raise His
voice in His defense. He did not hire a defense attorney.
Nor did He plan retaliation for those who participated in
His harsh treatment. No. He quietly accepted it all.

Having been found guilty of blasphemy, Jesus quietly
carried His cross to His place of death. It was there that
He suffered quietly on a cross for a bogus crime He had
not committed. There was no yelling. No protesting. No
bargaining. No crying. No panic praying. No. There was
nothing more than His quiet obedience.

And when Jesus was resurrected? Did He stand on a
mountaintop telling everyone He was alive? Did He shout
to all that He had been restored? That He, as the Son of
God, had cheated death?

No. Instead, Jesus quietly shows Himself to His disciples and to those who needed to see Him.

Let us imagine how Satan would have acted if he had been asked to endure the things Jesus was asked to endure. Being born in a manger. Living a quiet life in a foreign land such as Egypt. Having to slip away from a crowd who wanted to stone him. Being arrested in the garden. Would he really have reprimanded one of his own who tried to rescue him? And what about the mock trial and the harsh treatment? How would Satan have reacted to that? Then quietly carrying a cross to the place of his death where he would die for crimes he had not committed.

And then, should he be resurrected, do you really think he would not announce from a mountaintop that he was alive? Do you not think that he would boldly brag about how powerful he was? Brag that not even death could conquer him because he was so powerful!

Can you see Satan living though the same experiences Jesus did and exhibiting the same humility Jesus did? Can you envision Satan living with majestic power under total control?

Yeah ... Me neither.

If I Were a Hebrew Woman

Because some of Jesus's teachings were so different from what the church leaders, the Pharisees, were teaching at that time, I often ask myself this: If I had been a Hebrew woman during Jesus's time, would I have listened to what He had to say? That He was God's Son, the Messiah, whom we waited for? That He was my only way to heaven? That He and the heavenly Father were one? Or would I think He was a false teacher? Someone who was trying to harm my church? Someone to stay away from?

What would I have thought about His ability to heal others of their illnesses and disabilities? Or of the rumors that He had brought dead people back to life? And what about the stories of how He told the stormy seas to be stilled and they obeyed? And could He really walk on water? Not in it but on it. Are such stories true?

This man claimed to be the Son of God and even called God His heavenly Father. Would I think that this was blasphemy? Or the truth?

This man taught that we were to be humble and love our neighbor and yet He in a display of great anger shouted at vendors as He overturned tables at the temple.

He told us that He was our way to heaven. Our only way.

I would have heard that as He sat with His disciples, He called Himself the living bread stating that those who ate of His flesh and drank of His blood would abide in Him and He would abide in them.

> Then Jesus said them, "Most assuredly, I say to you, unless you eat the flesh of the Son of

Man and drink His blood, you have no life
in you. Whoever eats My flesh and drinks My
blood has eternal life, and I will raise him up
at the last day. For my flesh is food indeed,
and My blood is drink indeed. He who eats
My flesh and drinks My blood abides in Me,
and I in him." (John 6:53–56 NKJV)

And as if that were not enough, He called the Pharisees,
the leaders of my church, dead man's bones, a brood of
vipers, and hypocrites.

"Woe to you, scribes and Pharisees, hypocrites!
For you are like whitewashed tombs which
indeed appear beautiful outwardly, but
inside are full of dead men's bones and all
uncleanness." (Matthew 23:27 NKJV)

"Serpents, brood of vipers! How can you
escape the condemnation of hell?" (Matthew
23:33 NKJV)

Then Jesus called them children of Satan.

"You are of your father the devil, and the
desires of your father you want to do. He
was a murderer from the beginning and
does not stand in the truth, because there
is not truth in him. When he speaks a lie,
he speaks from his own resources, for he is
a liar and the father of it." (John 8:44 NKJV)

Would I have followed Him? Would I be found among the multitude hanging onto His every word? One of those who laid palms before Him during His entry into Jerusalem while crying out "Hosanna! Blessed is He who comes in the name of the LORD!"?

Or would I have been among the voices that cried "Crucify Him! Crucify Him!" Would I be found among the critics?

I am not a Hebrew woman during Jesus's time. However, I would love to say that if I had been, I would had poked out my chest and would have said with all assuredness, "Yes, I believe Jesus! And I'm going to follow Him!"

But knowing myself, I am not too sure I would have done so.

Thank you, Lord, for allowing me to be born now, at this time when I can hold and read the Father's Word telling me that such things are true. Thank you, Lord, that I will never have to be a Jewish girl facing such a decision.

Free Will

I have often wondered why God chose to give us free will. Us. The one creature He formed in His image.

Our pets and the animals that live in the wild seem to have some free will, but for the most part, they operate on instinct, which is God's usual way of doing things.

They instinctively know about things that we humans do not appear to know. Animals do not have to attend Lamaze classes to learn birthing their young. Nor do they attend parenting classes to learn how to parent. Moms and dads do a fine job of teaching their young ones how to hunt for food, how to fly, and how to stay safe from predators. They teach their offspring how to tell if a storm is coming and what to do when it hits. One thing I find awesome is how birds will teach their young to worship, to sing praise songs at sunrise.

But we humans, the only species He made in His image, were given strong and sometimes demanding free wills. Wouldn't it be so much easier if we lived by instinct with just a small amount of free will as animals do?

But God gave us free will because He loves us. If you try to force your children to do things and to love you, by removing their ability to make choices, they have no free will. And without some amount of free will, you cannot have mutual companionship. You cannot have an open and honest relationship. What you do have is called dictatorship. You are the dictator and your children the ones being dictated to.

But if you allow your children to exercise free will, to experience negative as well as positive consequences for their actions and choices, you will have a genuine relationship with them. There is no longer the dictator and dictated-to relationship. In its place is a parent-child relationship.

Children who are allowed a certain amount of free will learn to make good choices. They will learn that there are consequences for their actions—good and bad. They will learn to respect others. To give and take. To share.

Children who are allowed some free will are taught through leadership. Since they are no longer dictated to, they will be more willing to accept their parents as leaders. They will find stability in their parents' leadership roles and build a relationship with them based on that. Willingly. Leadership, not dictatorship, creates a desire to be with you. A desire to follow you. To please you.

The genuine feeling of love from this type of relationship will spark such things as communication, warmth, security, willing obedience, loyalty, and respect. Are these not the same things God desires from us? Is He not looking for us to lovingly respect and honor Him? To love Him? To be obedient? To be loyal?

That is why God gave us free will and not just instincts. He wants to be our heavenly Father, not our heavenly dictator. And when those who have free will choose to love Him, their love is freely given. By choice.

God wants us to choose to love, obey, and worship Him not because we have to or are being forced to but because we want to. Love, obedience, and worship given freely are genuine as well as sweet. God loves us so much that He wants to give us the ability to love Him in a genuine way. He wants to give us the ability to choose Him freely. So - He gave us free will.

David

As I was looking up scripture for this book, I realized that in the book of Psalms there are several chapters where David would ask for God's mercy; almost to the point of begging. He asked the Lord if He was listening to him. He asked the Lord to hear his cries.

> How long, O LORD? Will You forget me forever? How long will You hide Your face from me? (Psalm 13:1 NKJV)

David would often ask the Lord to protect him and to provide for his needs.

> Keep me as the apple of Your eye; hide me under the shadow of Your wings, from the wicked who oppress me, from my deadly enemies who surround me. (Psalm 17:8–9 NKJV)

And David would thank the Lord for His blessings.

> The king shall have joy in Your strength, O LORD; and in Your salvation how greatly shall he rejoice! You have given him his heart's desire and have not withheld the request of his lips. Selah. (Psalm 21:1–2 NKJV)

David would then sing praises to the Lord.

Give unto the LORD, O you mighty ones,
give unto the LORD glory and strength.
Give unto the LORD the glory due to His
name; worship the LORD in the beauty of
holiness. (Psalm 29:1–2 NKJV)

David was very open with the Lord about all aspects of his life. I think David's honesty with the Lord may be one reason the Lord found him pleasing. Why he was the apple of God's eye. Remember, our Lord already knows the truth. When we state otherwise without mouths, we are telling Him a lie. So please stay open and honest with God. For - He already God knows all things and see all things.

They Catch Behavior

I have heard many sermons regarding fathers and their roles in families. Good fathers who lovingly guide their children are as important as good mothers are. I have heard it said that children learn more by catching the behavior of their father.

Fathers influence the next generation of fathers who in turn influence the next generation of fathers and so on. Exodus 34:7 tells of the iniquities that pass from fathers to children and to their children. This influence can be either positive or negative. Healthy or unhealthy. Good or bad. Spirit filled or Satan filled.

Jesus Christ demonstrated such when He was on earth. He told us many times that what He said was not His words but those of the heavenly Father. And that His actions were not His actions but those of the heavenly Father. He told His disciples that He was in the Father and the Father was in Him. That He and the Father were one. That whoever saw Him saw the heavenly Father. And this was confirmed the moment Jesus was baptized.

Just how does Jesus model the heavenly Father?

1. He is the gardener who removes the branches that are not producing fruit.
2. He tells us how to live.
3. He gives us the house rules if you will.
4. He is merciful and just when we need it.
5. He understands our weaknesses.
6. He cares about what we care about.

7. He is a great listener.
8. He is fun loving.
9. He is only a prayer away always.
10. He is the giver of good gifts.
11. He protects us and provides us for we are His children.
12. He likes our obedience.
13. He is pleased when we rely on our faith in Him, for He is all knowing.
14. He wants only the best for us, His children.
15. He enjoys blessing His children.
16. He cares about what happens in His children's lives.
17. He cherishes the time He spends with His children. He loves us with all that He has and is.

The heavenly Father wants us to be with Him so much that He formatted a plan to cleanse our sins so that He could look upon us and live with us in the heavenly realm. He asked His one and only Son to die as our sacrificial sin Lamb so that through Jesus's blood, we could be viewed as one of the righteous in His eyes.

Big shoes to fill, huh, dads? But oh, what a great example!

Matthew 13

Then He spoke many things to them in parables, saying: "Behold, a sower went out to sow. And as he sowed, some seed fell by the wayside; and the birds came and devoured them. Some fell on stony places, where they did not have much earth; and they immediately sprang up because they had no depth of earth. But when the sun was up they were scorched, and because they had no root they withered away. And some fell among thorns, and the thorns sprang up and choked them. But others fell on good ground and yielded a crop; some a hundred-fold, some sixty, some thirty. He who has ears to hear, let him hear!" (Matthew 13:3–9 NKJV)

Ever wonder if the parable of the sower in Matthew 13 could be a guide for your spiritual study? This parable is about a farmer casting seed. Some of the seeds fell along the path. Some on the rocky road. Some among thorns. And some on good soil.

Some of the seeds were eaten by birds. Some were like a flash in the pan that burned away. Like plants with no grounding, they quickly withered. Some were choked out by weeds. But some fell on good ground and yielded great crops.

Let us look at this scripture just a little bit closer.

The farmer casting the seeds was Jesus. The seeds falling along the path were the times you did not listen to

God's Word when it was presented to you. The stony places were your life marked by a spasmodic study of God's Word. The thorns were the way that the world and its worries choked your faith in and knowledge of God.

And finally, we have the good soil, the daily study of God's Word while consistently seeking His guidance.

Jesus used this parable to warn us to stay off the rocky road, to stay in God's Word, and to talk with the Father about everything.

Allow the gospel to be absorbed by your roots—your head. Allow it to feed your vine—your soul. Allow it to cause your fruit—your spiritual heart—to grow and mature.

Your daily Bible study keeps your soil fertile. Plants need fertile soil to grow large and strong and not be as easily affected by thorns and weeds—worldly worries—as young and tender plants are.

But all this caring for and tending to takes time and work. For if the soil is not tended to, not kept fertile with daily fertilizer found in God's Word, the plants will not grow and will eventually die from the lack of care and from hunger before they can produce any fruit. Which is sad. Because others need to be fed from this fruit. And now, they will never know just how sweet this fruit once was.

He who has ears, let him hear!

Master and Lord

I love my two dogs very much. To them, I am their master, the lord of their lives. I can tell them what they are allowed to do, where they are allowed to go, and when they can. But as their lord, I also have the responsibility of caring for them; I am to make sure they have food, fresh water, a warm bed to sleep in, and proper housing. I am to watch over them and make sure they don't get into things such as toxic frogs or poisonous snakes.

In response to my care my dogs bark when someone comes in the gate. They guard against the intrusion of squirrels, rabbits, and such as I go about my outside chores. I believe they would give up their lives to protect me from an attacker if the need arose. My dogs do these things willingly and enthusiastically.

They willingly obey such commands as "In" while I point to their crate. Or "Come" when I need for them to be at my side.

My dogs do their part, and I do mine; we're a team.

Let's relate their behavior to your behavior with God. Have you made God the Lord of your life? Is He really your Master? Have you asked His Son, Jesus Christ, to be your Savior? To be your lifeline to God? If not, why not?

If you have, then is God not the Lord of your life? And as your Lord, does He not have the right to tell you what to do? How to do Where to go? And when to go?

As the Lord of your life, God will make sure you have food, fresh water, a warm bed, and proper housing. He will watch over you and guide you. He will warn you of the toxic toads and poisonous snakes that may lie along your path. He promised to take care of you, and He will do what He promised to do.

As the Master of your life, God will give you work to do for Him. He may ask you to take someone to the grocery store or help someone clean his or her house. Or maybe even ask you to preach some sermons to His people. And just how do you do the jobs He gives you? Willingly and with great enthusiasm. To the best of your ability.

When God points to your crate and says, "In," do you enter your crate in anticipation of a treat? Or do you enter the crate just because God asked you to? If you were to take an honest look at your motives for doing the things God asks you to do, what would you find? Would you be doing them because you are thankful to God for His gift of salvation through Jesus Christ? So thankful that you just can't do enough for Him? Or is there another motive?

While you are looking into the mirror of honesty, are you always obedient to God? Do you always do as He asks you to do?

No? Well, that's okay. My dogs aren't either. But I still love them. And God still loves you.

> Cast your cares on the LORD and he will sustain you; he will never let the righteous fall. (Psalm 55:22 NIV)

Facing a Storm

Yesterday morning, my husband and I awoke to an incoming storm which is good news. We had not had any rain for at least seven to ten days, and the rain that we did have was only a fleeting shower. Plants are suffering. Lawns are brown. Neighbors are fighting with each other over how much water is being used. Florida without rain is not a pretty sight.

As we dressed for the day, we listened to news warning of severe weather. Along with the much-needed rain, there will be strong winds, blinding rain, dangerous lightning, and even possible tornadoes. And the storms were due within the next two hours which is about the time we would normally be leaving for work. So, we decided to leave for work twenty minutes early.

On the way to work, I saw the storm's oncoming shelf cloud. The big, dark, ominous storm cloud grew larger as it raced toward me. Then the rain came. Softly at first becoming harder. And harder. A strong headwind gusted against my vehicle. Lightning was popping around me. The morning sky had blackened and resembled a night sky, which enhanced the intense streaks of lightning. I had driven right into the thing I wanted to avoid. The storm.

My windshield wipers are on high, but they were no match for the deluge. Driving with both hands is necessary due to the strong winds that are pushing my small car over into the next lane. I cannot see anything ahead or behind me. It was as if I am the only car on the road. The only thing I can see are the reflectors between the two lanes. Following them should guarantee that I stay in my lane.

As long as I d0 not hear a crunch, I will know that I have not run over anything.

Arggh! I do not like driving in such storms. Since I cannot tell where I am, safely pulling over and waiting out the storm does not seem an option. Fear starts to creep in, and I began to shake. So I pray "Oh Lord, please be with me. Help me. Guide me. And forgive me for being so afraid."

And then, as if in response to my prayer, scripture came to me. It was the scripture I had read the night before. Scripture about the parting of the Red Sea. As I faced my Red Sea, I thought about how frightened the Israelites must have been. They are stuck between an Egyptian army bent on destroying them, and the Red Sea. I am quite sure they were physically shaking with fear just as I was. And I am quite sure they were thinking that they were going to die. How could they not?

Moses, a great man of God, went to the Lord for help. For guidance. For direction. Moses had faith in God's ability, and because of his faith, an entire nation saw a great move of God's hand. They saw a sea parted. With huge amounts of water pulled back on their left and on their right, they walked on land that was once covered with this sea but is now dry. And then, as if God put a cherry on top of His grace cake, once the Israelites had crossed the Red Sea, God allowed the waters to return to their original home drowning the Egyptian army in the process. The Israelites lived to tell this story to their children, to their children's children, and so on. All because of the faith on one man.

Wow!

My thoughts returned to my present situation. I was still

driving in a bad storm filled with strong winds, blinding rain, and fierce lightning. However, the storm, as bad as it was, was no comparison to what the Israelites had faced. Odd how this thought seemed to give me the strength to go on. The strength to continue driving in this severe thunderstorm. This remembrance of what God had done for His children instilled a renewed confidence in how God can and *will* take care of me. As I allowed that fact to sink deep down into my soul, my confidence grew. Which in turned allowed me to boldly face the storm.

Was I now allowing God to direct my path? Or was God removing my fear? I'm not sure. But in my mind's eye, I could see God parting my Red Sea. I see angels around me protecting me and guiding me. Oh, how merciful and loving our God is!

Was it a coincidence that I had read that scripture the night before I needed to draw on while in a storm? I don't think so. The Lord knew that I would be driving through this storm, so He had guided me to this part of His Word. For you see, when you're living life with God, there are no coincidences.

The next time you drive into a storm be it weather related or life related, remember the parting of the Red Sea. Remember God's willingness to care for you. If you are a child of God, He will take care of you; He has promised to care for His own. And God always keeps His promises.

God is our refuge and strength, a very present help in trouble. (Psalm 46:1 NKJV)

The LORD is your keeper; the LORD is your shade at your right hand. The sun shall not strike you by day, nor the moon by night.

The LORD shall preserve you from all evil;
He shall preserve your soul. The LORD shall
preserve your going out and your coming in
from this time forth, and even forevermore.
(Psalm 121:5–8 NKJV)

Reflectors

Living the Christian life can be equated to driving down a country road. It may be a road that you have traveled frequently or one you've never been on. At times, you will be driving a straight stretch and seeing what lies ahead for miles. Times when the travel is so easy it seems as though your car is driving itself.

And then there will be times when the road is filled with all kinds of curves, narrow lanes, potholes, and obstacles. Times when you need to have both hands on the wheel. Times when your car seems to be drifting or slowing down just to speed up again.

The illumination of the road that we are driving on will vary as well. Sometimes, there will be a full moon which lights up the road and allows you full view of what is ahead of you. But then there will be other times when the moon is in a new phase and is giving off no light. You can barely see past the hood of your car even with your headlights on. It is on these dark nights that we must look for illumination from another source.

There will be the times when we must travel our road on stormy nights. When our car is being pounded by strong winds, and unrelenting rain in total darkness. On such nights, only the reflectors found in the road will tell us whether the road is straight or curving. And if we are to drive safely in such conditions, we must follow their lead. But - for the reflectors to do their job, we must first turn on our headlights. The reflectors rely on the external light that emits from our headlights. Reflectors cannot reflect unless they have a light source.

I have noticed that the darker the night or the more intense the storm, the better the reflectors work. And the better they work, the more I rely on them. The light they reflect seems to be more brilliant on those dark, stormy nights, when we need them the most.

And so, it is with our road of life as Christians. There will be times when our travel is straight, smooth, easy. And then there will be times when we need to rely on the reflectors of our lives. Times when we need to turn our headlights on.

If you have a relationship with Jesus, then you have what you need to navigate those treacherous roads. Those stormy drives. For you have Jesus and He is your light source. And He has given you the Holy Spirit who is your reflector. Then He promised to never leave you – **never.** Which means they will be there to guide you around the tightest hairpin curves in the worst storms – **always.**

Guaranteed.

> Then Jesus spoke to them again, saying, "I am the light of the world. He who follows Me shall not walk in darkness, but have the light of life." (John 8:12 NKJV)

Discipline—Yuck!

> My son, do not despise the chastening of the
> LORD, nor detest His correction; for whom
> the LORD loves He corrects, just as a father
> the son in whom he delights. (Proverbs 3:11–
> 12 NKJV)

No one likes to be disciplined. It is awkward, embarrassing,
and often painful. However, discipline is necessary.
Without discipline, without chastening, the correct way
of living cannot be known. Discipline helps us learn the
value of correct actions, of correct speech, and of correct
thoughts, but they must be taught. And so, it is with the
ways of God.

When we first became Christians, we were called baby
Christians because we needed to grow in our faith and
mature as Christians. The moment we accepted Jesus
Christ as our Lord and Savior. We became joint heirs with
Him making His heavenly Father our heavenly Father. We
become God's children.

> For as many as are led by the Spirit of God,
> these are sons of God. For you did not
> receive the spirit of bondage again to fear,
> but you received the Spirit of adoption by
> whom we cry out, "Abba, Father." The Spirit
> Himself bears witness with our spirit that we
> are children of God, and if children, then
> heirs—heirs of God and joint heirs with
> Christ, if indeed we suffer with Him, that

we may also be glorified together. (Romans 8:14–17 NKJV)

Newborns are fed nothing more that milk for their first few months. But once they grow a bit, their diets become more varied and much more nourishing. And so, it is with Christians. Hebrews 5:12 -13 talks about the spiritually immature partaking of only milk, while those who are mature feed on solid food.

Children learn the ways of life from their parents. They learn to walk and talk. What they can play with and what is not to be touched. Their parents teach them with love and mercy and discipline. However, good parents use discipline only when needed and administer it with love. They know what their children must learn to be safe and to function well in life. And so, it is with God's children.

As children mature and become older, their parents must adjust the way they teach and guide them. Older children need different discipline applied in a different manner. Time-out in the corner of a room is much more effective for a six-year-old than it is for a sixteen-year-old. And the loss of driving privileges is not nearly as important to a six-year-old as it is to a sixteen-year-old. And so, it is with God's children.

As children mature and become older, they can understand more and are able to apply wisdom differently. Older children can understand and accept more-complex theories. They will also have an increased ability to understand reason. They will have a better ability to wait on anticipated events. And so, it is with God's children.

Discipline breeds wisdom. And wisdom breeds discipline. It also strengthens us and prepares us for future work. Just ask anyone who has been in the military. First comes boot camp to instill discipline. Then comes the training that feeds off that instilled discipline. Finally, when all is in order, the actual work detail is added.

As God's children spiritually mature and begin to see God in a different light, their lives change. And so does their discipline and the way it is tendered. As God's children mature, their capacity to understand His ways improve. As their knowledge of God grows, so will their ability to apply it to life.

We will never understand all of God's ways, which are higher than ours. But the more spiritually mature we become, the more we will listen to the Holy Spirit. And the more we listen to the Holy Spirit, the more we will see God's hand at work and understand His actions. We will learn to wait on Him and have a childlike faith in Him.

God takes us as newborn Christians and lovingly guides along the path of life. He tenderly teaches us His ways through His Word, where we find Bible stories and the teachings of His Son, Jesus Christ. God will answer our questions and calms our fears.

Just as earthly fathers do, He disciplines us for He loves us and wants us to stay safe. God knows our adversary, Satan. God knows how deceptive Satan is and the dangers that await us should we make the wrong choices.

God wants us to mature as Christians. He wants us to know Him and His ways. He wants us to use the gifts He has given us to their fullest and to succeed. He wants us to mature into strong Christians who can help the newborn or baby Christians effectively.

And when we do, the entire cycle begins again.

Husbands and Wives

Our Bibles are our owner's manuals for how to live life. They have instructions from God on how to handle anything that comes our way. Things like how to manage money, how to have great relationships, and how to live righteous lives. Our Bibles also give us advice about that institution between a man and a woman—marriage.

While the Word tells us that marriage creates a union between husband and wife, sometimes, the stress and cares of life can create deep cavities in that union. If we turn to God's Word for help during those seasons, we will find instructions on how to remove the cavities and have happy and productive marriages. Yes, just like the repairing of physical cavities in our teeth, this transition from brokenness to oneness can and will be painful. But also like the repairing of our teeth, it is so worth it.

Wives are instructed to submit to their husbands. Yes! I know there is that word *submit*, and just like you, I don't like submitting to anyone. But God tells wives to submit to the authority of their husbands in all things. Not in just some things but in all things. Unless her husband is asking her to do something that is against God's law or to do something that is harmful to her welfare such as jumping off a bridge, the wife is to submit to her husband's God-given authority in the home. Bottom line, ladies.

And she has been instructed to respect her husband as she submits. (So, no rolling your eyes here, ladies!) For the Lord has made the husband to be the head of the home. And because of his God-given role, the wife is to respect her husband as that head of the home. *Period.*

> Wives, submit to your own husbands, as unto
> the Lord. For the husband is head of the
> wife, as also Christ is head of the church;
> and he is the Savior of the body. Therefore,
> just as the church is subject to Christ, so
> let the wives be to their own husbands in
> everything. (Ephesians 5:22–24 NKJV)

However, please remember, ladies, that with authority comes responsibility. And the greater the authority, the greater the responsibility. Because God gave your husband the authority as the spiritual leader of your home, God also gave your husband the responsibility of being the spiritual leader of your home.

I am treading in an area that some women can get touchy about. So let me state that nowhere in my Bible have I ever found it said or even indicated that women are to be doormats. That women are to be servants to their husbands waiting on them hand and foot fulfilling their every command. No. I have found in my Bible that wives are to be helpers to their husbands. God created woman to be a companion and a helper.

> And the LORD God said, "It is not good that
> man should be alone; I will make him a helper
> comparable to him." Out of the ground the
> LORD God formed every beast of the field
> and every bird of the air, and brought them
> to Adam to see what he would call them. And
> whatever Adam called each living creature,
> that was its name. So Adam gave names to
> all cattle, to the birds of the air, and to every

beast of the field. But for Adam there was not found a helper comparable to him.

And the LORD God caused a deep sleep to fall upon Adam, and he slept; and He took one of his ribs, and closed up the flesh in its place. Then the rib which the LORD God had taken from man He made into a woman, and He brought her to the man. (Genesis 2:18–22 NKJV)

God made woman to be man's helper who was comparable to him. And as comparable helpers to their husbands, wives may voice their opinions when decisions of life are to be made. If I read God's Word correctly, the wife's opinion is just as important as the husband's. For the wife is to be her husband's helper, she is to warn him of any upcoming dangers she may see. Or perhaps she may show him an easier way to do something.

Wives are allowed and even encouraged to be self-starters. Great thinkers. Hard workers. Proverbs 31 tells us that wives are to be business owners and owners of land. They are to be mangers of people. Mothers to their children. The woman I see in Proverbs 31 is one of good, strong moral character. No doormats here, ladies!

Check out Proverbs 31 for yourself.

So, wives, may I gently ask you for some self-evaluation. How are you treating you husbands? Are you treating them with the respect God has asked of you? Do they always have your submission in all things? Do you honor them as the heads of your households? Are you being the comparable helpers God created you to be?

Or do you speak to them in disrespectful tones? Are

your tongues sharp? Do you pout when you don't get your way? Are you argumentative? Manipulative? Not completely honest all the time? Stingy with your feelings? Do you withdraw? Are you an ice queen?

In Ephesians, husbands were instructed to love their wives so much that they would be willing to lay down their lives for their wives. They were told to nurture them and care for them. Husbands are to provide their wives not just with food and housing, but spiritually as well.

> Husbands, love your wives, just as Christ also loved the church and gave Himself for her, that he might sanctify and cleanse her with the washing of water by the word, that He might present her to Himself a glorious church, not having spot or wrinkle or any such thing, but that she should be holy and without blemish. So husbands ought to love their own wives as their own bodies; he who loves his wife loves himself. (Ephesians 5:25–28 NKJV)

When a husband loves his wife as though she were his own body, then it is easy for the wife to accept her husband's authority in the home. And – when the woman accepts her husband's authority in the home, it is easy for her husband to love her as he does his own body.

The Fourth of July

The Fourth of July. What a colorful holiday with fireworks filling the night sky. All I have to do to see fireworks is to step out my back door. For I live in the country. And this year was no exception.

After a short time of fireworks watching, I noticed one of my horses, Molly, was stressing out. The fire raining from the sky followed by loud noises seemed to be too much. She had worked herself up to a point that was close to panic mode and had actually run into a wooden fence. *Hmmm.* Time to see if I could help her.

When I stepped out into her paddock, my other horse, Sonny, saw me and decided to join me. He came over to the fence and stood as close to me as the fence would allow him to. Molly in the other hand was still running around in panic mode.

I reached over the fence to scratch Sonny and started singing. Horses find music soothing. (And they do not care what you sound like. You can sing off key, sing the wrong words, or even make some up.) Leaning into the fence for a better scratch, Sonny picked up his ears and listened to my songs. His body began to lose its tenseness, and he was chewing. Chewing is a sign of relaxation.

Encouraged by Sonny's positive responses, I continued to sing. And then I felt it. Molly's breath on my neck. She too was listening to my songs. So, I turned to console her the best I could. Frightened horses can be difficult and sometimes dangerous to those around them. They can experience stress colic, which can be, and often is, life threatening. Quieting Molly was a must. So I continued stroking Sonny and singing.

My presence, Sonny's relaxed mood and singing helped Molly. She began to respond in a positive way. Her body was beginning to relax, she had dropped her head and blew out a huge breath of air. All are signs of relaxation. This lasted until the next loud noise came followed by fire raining from the sky. Then it was back to panic mode and off she ran.

As I continued to stand there in the paddock close to Sonny, he began to watch the fireworks with me. And I praised him for his bravery. Which in turn increased his confidence and made him braver. Now he was standing beside me with confidence. I praised him for his proper response, which increased his confidence even more.

And then there was poor Molly. Still running away from the scary stuff. Still in panic mode. Still running into wooden fences.

Slowly but surely, my singing and Sonny's newly found bravery was beginning to influence Molly. She saw Sonny standing next to me relaxed, confident and watching the fireworks, and gradually became less fearful. With less fear, she realized that the loud noises and raining fire were not harming him. Funny how her fear caused short-term blindness.

Molly started running only a short distance away. This short distance became even shorter and shorter, until she was actually standing behind me. I was so proud of her. She may have placed me between herself and the monsters, but at least she was standing there with me. Even if it was behind me.

By the end of the night, Sonny and Molly and I were

just hanging out in the paddock watching what was left of our fireworks show. And everyone was quiet and calm.

Hmmm. Reminds me of something.

In the paddock, I was a quiet and consistent influence, which helped my horses handle their fear. They began to trust that I would be with them in the fearfulness of loud noises and fire raining down. The more consistent I was, the more their fear lessened. Their attempts to run away were fewer and shorter. And the desire to hide from the monsters subsided as well. There was no more fear of the unknown.

This is how God is in our lives.

Sonny and Molly knew my voice. And they perked their ears my way so they could listen to my voice as I sang to them. They found my voice soothing and comforting.

This is how God's voice is to us.

I could stand in the paddock in a very confident manner because I knew that we were not in extreme danger. I knew what the outcome of this event would be.

And God knows the same about our lives.

Sonny was the first of the two to start responding. He was the first to believe that I was there to help him and that I would protect him if needed. He was the first to stand next to me even if he was afraid at first. He was a great example of a Christian who is fully trusting God.

Funny how a horse can be a better example of what a trusting Christian looks like than I do at times. How a horse can show me what trusting God should look like. I am the one who was made in the image of God. The one who runs around telling others just how much I trust in God. Not the horse.

Molly, however, was just the opposite. She was running

around in panic mode. She was allowing her fear to take over and to keep her from seeing where her help was. And then once she did find help, she continued allowing her fear to rob her of the trust in that help. Molly did what so many of us do when we do not take our fears to God. When we do not allow God to help us with our fears. When we do not trust in His willingness to take care of us while we are in that fearful situation. In that panic mode.

At times, we stand by God all brave and all mighty saying, "It's you and me, God! You and me!" That is until we become frightened because of the loud noises and fireworks raining down in our lives. Then we tend to run away from God, the only one who can really help us. We want to hide in the darkness because this was where we hid from scary things before, we met Jesus.

And that is okay. God is patient with us. He will stand there in the paddock quietly waiting for us to come back to Him for as long as it takes. And He will do it again and again. He will wait for us to come to Him. To trust Him. To decide that the safest place to be is standing beside Him. And when we do, we will find confidence, relaxation and rest in His presence even if the loud noises and fireworks are still there.

When we turn to God for help with our fears, we will find His presence quiet and consistent. His voice will be soothing and comforting. He will be a stabilizing force for us every time we turn to Him. *Every time.*

> Have I not commanded you? Be strong and of good courage; do not be afraid, nor be dismayed, for the LORD your God is with you where you go. (Joshua 1:9 NKJV)

The Week before Easter

This is the week before Easter. How exciting! And there is so much to be done. Let's go down the list.

1. House cleaning before guests arrive.
2. Easter eggs to dye for the Easter egg hunt.
3. Grocery shopping for the Easter Day meal.
4. And do not forget those nice chocolate treats that come only at Easter like the chocolate bunnies and the colored eggs. (Yummy)

You work hard preparing for one of the most important days for a Christian. Then the day arrives. After the sunrise service, you rush home to put the ham on and handle the final preparations. Is everything in place? Whew! So much to do!

The first week before Easter was quite busy for Jesus as well. There was the donkey ride into town and the cleansing of God's temple. Jesus healed those who were blind and lame and cursed a fig tree. He spoke to a crowd, who heard a voice from heaven. A woman used her hair to anoint Jesus with expensive perfume while at the home of Simon, the leper. He sat down at the Feast of the Unleavened Bread to eat the Last Supper with His disciples during which He had communion with them. They then sang a song. Afterward, Jesus set about washing the feet of each one of His twelve.

After the Last Supper, Jesus went to the Mount of Olives, where He prayed fervently to His heavenly Father asking Him to remove the cup that had been given Him.

After His Father did not remove the cup, Jesus accepted the will of His heavenly Father, was attended to by angels, and prayed for His disciples. He woke up His sleeping followers and went out to meet those who were there to arrest Him.

Jesus was then betrayed by one of His disciples with a kiss. When asked if He was Jesus the Nazarene, His answer caused all to fall to the ground. He then healed the ear that Simon Peter cut off and scolded Peter for such actions. Jesus was then arrested by the Jews and bound by a detachment of troops.

After His arrest, Jesus went before Pilate, who after listening to Jesus sent Him to stand before Herod. After finding no fault in Jesus, Herod sent Him back to Pilate, who had Him beaten and flogged almost to death. In mockery of His royalty, a crown of thorns was placed on His head. Being accused and falsely found guilty of blasphemy, Jesus stood before a mob of people who were crying "Crucify Him!" for they chose the release of Barabbas over Jesus. Like any good politician, Pilate gave the people what they wanted and agreed to have Jesus crucified even though Herod had said that he had found no reason to do so.

After being tormented and tortured, Jesus was given a heavy wooden cross to carry to a place called Golgotha. A place where He was stripped down and nailed to the cross. He was mocked. Laughed at. Guards gambled for His clothing. Onlookers watched as life drained from His mortal body. His mourning relatives looked on. Even as His dying body was hanging on the cross, Jesus took care of His mother's welfare. He saved the soul. For the criminal who was being crucified with Him recognized who Jesus was and asked Jesus to take him to heaven with

Him. And He told the criminal, "Truly you will be with Me in paradise."

Then Jesus asked His heavenly Father to forgive the people who had beaten Him. Flogged Him. Laughed at Him. Mocked Him. Falsely accused Him. Had yelled, "Crucify Him!" Had nailed Him on the cross by driving spikes into His body. Yes, even those people.

As His body grew weaker, Jesus spoke His last words to the heavenly Father and then died. At this very second, at the time of His death, Jesus became our sacrificial Sin Lamb. Our blood sacrifice for all of our sin, past, present, and future. For all people. For all of time.

Scripture tells us that unless there is a blood sacrifice, there cannot be remission of sin. Jesus was not only the blood sacrifice that covered our sins; He was the blood sacrifice that ended the need for all blood sacrifices. Never again would man have to go to the Temple to offer up a blood sacrifice for their sin. Jesus's Blood covers that.

> And according to the law almost all things are purified with blood, and without shedding of blood there is no remission. (Hebrews 9:22 NKJV)

But Jesus's work was not done. Three days later, He rose from death. His body resurrected. Fulfilling Old Testament prophesy, Jesus arose from death and went to be with His disciples and with others. Until He was taken up into Heaven.

It was the week before Easter. Whew! Jesus had so much to do.

Why Should You Pay Taxes?

Tax season is upon us. It seems as if we work hard just to support our federal government, doesn't it? And to add fuel to that fire, we are not always happy with the way the government spends our money. Most of us must live in a very thrifty way, but our government tends to live in an extravagant way. In light of this, you may find it extremely easy to fudge the numbers on your tax return just a bit. Or be smug about that purchase for which you skirted sales tax.

But let me ask you, my fellow Christian, what did Jesus say about paying taxes?

> "Tell us, therefore, what do You think? Is it lawful to pay taxes to Caesar, or not?" But Jesus perceived their wickedness, and said, "Why do you test Me you hypocrites?"
>
> "Show Me the tax money." So they brought Him a denarius. And He said to them, "Whose image and inscription is this?" They said to Him, "Caesar's." And He said to them, "Render therefore to Caesar the things that are Caesar's and to God the things that are God's." (Matthew 22:17–21 NKJV)

So why should you pay taxes? Outside of the fact that you do not cherish the IRS dipping into your bank accounts, or the possibility of jail time does not rate as your dream vacation, why should you pay taxes? Jesus told us to pay to Caesar what belongs to him.

We should pay taxes because God told us to. And He told us to not once but at least twice. According to the book of Romans, those who are in governmental offices are in those offices because God wants them to be there. They are doing the work that God wants them to do, even if it is without their knowledge.

Check out this scripture.

> Let every soul be subject to the governing authorities. For there is no authority except from God, and the authorities that exist are appointed by God. Therefore whoever resists the authority resists the ordinance of God, and those who resist will bring judgment on themselves. For rulers are not a terror to good works, but to evil. Do you want to be unafraid of the authority? Do what is good, and you will have praise from the same. For he is God's minister to you for good.

> But if you do evil, be afraid; for he does not bear the sword in vain; for he is God's minister; an avenger to execute wrath on him who practices evil. Therefore you must be subject, not only because of wrath but also for conscience sake.

> For because of this you also pay taxes, for they are God's minister attending continually to this very thing. Render therefore to all their due: taxes to whom taxes are due, customs

to whom customs, fear to whom fear, honor
to whom honor. (Romans 13:1–7 NKJV)

We enable those who are in office to remain in office
by paying our taxes. How they handle the money we pay
them be it good or bad is something they will have to
answer to God for. Romans tells us that anyone who rebels
against what God has instituted will bring judgment on
themselves. Whoever does evil needs to be afraid.

God's Word is telling us that we bring judgment on
ourselves when we resist His ordinances. And, according
to what Jesus taught, we are to render unto Caesar what is
Caesar's and to God what is God's. We Christians are held
to a higher standard; we are to be honest in all things,
living in great integrity. Which means no lying in any way,
shape, or form.

So why must you pay taxes? Because God tells you to.
Bottom line.

Family Resemblance

We all have some resemblance to members of our families. There is always some type of family trait. Blond hair. Blue eyes. Height. Tipped-up noses. Maybe no nose at all. (he-he. Just joking.)

Sons resemble their fathers. Daughters have their mother's facial expressions. Some may have more than others and others less. But we all do have at least some resemblances to others in our families.

And so, it was with Jesus and the heavenly Father. He repeatedly told the people of His day that He and the Father were one. That whoever looked upon Him also looked upon God. For God was His Father and He was God's Son.

I and My Father are one. (John 10: 30 NKJV)

At Jesus's baptism, God confirmed who Jesus has said. He told those who were that Jesus was His Son whom He loved and was well pleased with Him.

When He had been baptized, Jesus came up immediately from the water; and behold the heavens were opened to Him, and He saw the Spirit of God descending like a dove and alighting upon Him. And suddenly a voice came from heaven, saying, "This is My beloved Son, in whom I am well pleased." (Matthew 3:16–17 NKJV)

Since this is so, by looking at Jesus's behavior, we can learn about God's behavior. In the New Testament, we see Jesus having compassion for those who were disabled or ill. We see Jesus tending to the needs of others and washing the feet of His disciples at the Last Supper. He calmed their fears on stormy seas. He was tender with the Samaritan woman at the well and was just as openly angry at the money changers in the temple. He stood His ground with Satan in the desert. Taught those who would listen. Fed those who were hungry. Protected children. Healed those who were afflicted. Rid tormented souls of demonic spirits. Brought back life from death. Communicated with His Father. And loved everybody.

Jesus, the one and only Son of God, showed us the traits of the one and only Father. Family members have family traits. God has compassion for those who are disabled or ill. He tends to His children. He calms fears. He welcomes the outcast. Has anger toward injustice. Is tender with the broken. Teaches those who will listen. Feeds those who are hungry. Heals those who are afflicted. Enjoys hearing from His children. And loves us all – very much.

> Thank You, Jesus, for showing us a glimpse
> of the heavenly Father.

What a Contrast

We have been told about Jesus's soft and loving side. About how He loves you and me. How He healed the sick. Rescued those who were doomed to hell. Gave sight to the blind and the ability to walk to the lame. Jesus talked with those who were rejected by society. Outcasts if you will. He was very willing to show His humbleness by washing the feet of His disciples and by spending time with tax collectors.

Jesus walked among men encouraging them to live in peace. To sincerely love one another. He had the power of God at His beck and call, but at times, He chose not to use it. Instead, He chose to be an example of how a humble person was to live. The word *humble* indicates that there is a great power being kept under control.

One of the few times Jesus stood before a crowd claiming to be who He was—the Messiah, the Son of God—was in the garden when the Pharisees came to arrest Him. Otherwise, Jesus quietly carried His cross to His place of death. He suffered quietly on the cross. There was no attempted escape. No yelling. No protesting. No whining. No panic praying. Only quiet obedience unto death.

And when He was resurrected, did Jesus stand on the top of a mountain announcing to all who would see Him that He was back? That though they had tried to kill Him, they had failed. Did He go around showing everyone His hands and feet and boasting about how He had been restored? No. He quietly showed Himself to those who needed to see Him. To those who needed to see His resurrected body.

Jesus was such a picture of great power under control.

A magnitude of power that is far beyond our imagination. As one of my favorite Easter songs goes, He could have called 10,000 angels to come and minister to his physical pain as He hung on the cross. And yet He allowed His suffering to continue. And He did so willingly.

But the scriptures also show us that there was another side to Jesus. A firm side. A side that was not afraid to tell the truth when it was needed. A side that would not tolerate sin. A side that could not endure those who were taking advantage of others by manipulating events. Especially when the manipulators were leaders and teachers. Men who were respected and had authority over the people.

Men like the Pharisees. Jesus did not tolerate their behavior or back down when they confronted Him. Instead, Jesus threw over the tables and benches of those who were dishonest money changers and dove sellers calling them robbers.

> Then Jesus went into the temple of God and drove out all those who bought and sold in the temple, and overturned the tables of the money changers and the seats of those who sold doves. And He said to them, "It is written, 'My house shall be called a house of prayer,' but you have made it a 'den of thieves.'" (Matthew 21:12–13 NKJV)

Jesus not only called the Pharisees blind guides and hypocrites, He told them that they were destined for hell.

> "Woe to you, scribes and Pharisees, hypocrites! For you travel land and sea to

win one proselyte, and when he is won, you make him twice as much a son of hell as yourselves." (Matthew 23:15 NKJV)

And that they were taking the church with them.

"But woe to you, scribes and Pharisees, hypocrites! For you shut up the kingdom of heaven against men; for you neither go in yourselves, nor do you allow those who are entering to go in." (Matthew 25:13 NKJV)

Jesus called them greedy and self-indulgent.

"But all their works they do to be seen by men. They make their phylacteries broad and enlarge the borders of their garments. They love the best places at feasts, the best seats in the synagogues, greetings in the marketplaces, and to be called by men, 'Rabbi, Rabbi'." (Matthew 23:5 NKJV)

Jesus scolded them for neglecting the important matters of the law such as justice, mercy, and faithfulness. Jesus said:

"Woe to you, teachers of the law and Pharisees, you hypocrites! You give a tenth of your spices – mint, dill and cumin. But you have neglected the more important matters of the law – justice, mercy and faithfulness. You should have practiced the latter, without neglecting the former. You blind guides!

You strain out a gnat but swallow a camel."
(Matthew 23:23–24 NIV)

Jesus told the Pharisees that they were like whitewashed tombs that looked beautiful on the outside but were filled with the bones of dead men. Jesus said:

> "Woe to you, teachers of the law and Pharisees, your hypocrites! You are like whitewashed tombs, which look beautiful on the outside but on the inside are full of dead men's bones and everything unclean. In the same way, on the outside you appear to people as righteous but on the inside you are full of hypocrisy and wickedness."
> (Matthew 23:27–28 NIV)

Jesus called them a brood of vipers. A brood of snakes who are condemned to hell. Jesus said:

> "You snakes! You brood of vipers! How will you escape being condemned to hell?"
> (Matthew 23:33 NIV)

Then Jesus exposes the Pharisees for who they were—Satan's children.

> Jesus said to them, "If God were your Father, you would love me, for I came from God and now am here. I have not come on my own; but he sent me. Why is my language not clear to you? Because you are unable to hear what I say. You belong to your father,

the devil, and you want to carry out your father's desire. He was a murderer from the beginning, not holding to the truth, for there is no truth in him. When he lies, he speaks his native language, for he is a liar and the father of lies. Yet because I tell the truth, you do not believe me! Can any of you prove me guilt of sin? If I am telling the truth, why don't you believe me? He who belongs to God hears what God says. The reason you do not hear is that you do not belong to God." (John 8:42–47 NIV)

Whew! Jesus was not always the soft-spoken teacher we have grown to know Him as. He may even have raised His voice some as He addressed the Pharisees. Jesus had great power. He told us that He and God were one. That if we knew Him, we knew God. That if we knew God, we knew Him. Jesus had access to the power of God. He was filled with God's power.

Jesus still has that same great power today. He is still able to heal, provide for, and protect His own. He gave you some of His power the moment you accepted Him as your Savior, the instant you received Him as your sacrificial Lamb for your sins. The moment you were bathed in His blood, you received forgiveness and the Holy Spirit. You now have a power source that you can tap into whenever you need it. Wherever you need it. Day or night. Holidays included. Anytime.

Now that's what I call a win-win.

Go, Jonah!

Our pastor had been teaching us from the book of Jonah. We heard, read, and learned about Jonah's rebellion toward God. About how his rebellion was the reason he was swallowed by a big fish. And about God's mercy on him.

Jonah was openly rebellious with God. When I read about how he tried to run away and hide from God, I asked myself, "*What was he thinking? How could Jonah hide from God? How could anyone hide from God?*"

When Jonah tried to run from God, He had a large fish swallow Jonah, and Jonah remained in its belly for three days and three nights. While in that situation, Jonah feared for his life and prayed to God for His mercy.

> But the LORD provided a great fish to swallow Jonah, and Jonah was inside the fish three days and three nights. From inside the fish Jonah prayed to the LORD his God. (Jonah 1:17–2:1 NIV)

However, Jonah's rebellion did not stop there. Jonah eventually did what God had asked him to do, but he did so with the greatest of protest. He certainly did not have warm fuzzies in his heart as he went to Nineveh, nor did he have a love for the people of Nineveh. Jonah could have been rolling his eyes as he traveled to Nineveh, a wicked nation filled with wicked people. And when God showed mercy to Nineveh, Jonah actually became angry with God. Yes! Just a few verses ago, Jonah was in the belly of the fish, begging for God's mercy. But then when God showed mercy to the people of Nineveh, he became angry.

Jonah did as God had asked him to do, but his heart was not with the people of Nineveh who had turned from God. However, we do see that Jonah learned his fish lesson well and obeyed God.

> Then the word of the LORD came to Jonah a second time: "Go to the great city of Nineveh and proclaim to it the message I give you." Jonah obeyed the word of the LORD and went to Nineveh. Now Nineveh was a very important city—a visit required three days. (Jonah 3:1–3 NIV)

Because of Jonah's obedience, a nation was saved. Although Jonah may have been rolling his eyes while he warned Nineveh, in doing so he saved it. Many listened to and believed what Jonah had to say. Even the king of Nineveh was touched.

> On the first day, Jonah started into the city. He proclaimed: "Forty more days and Nineveh will be overturned." The Ninevites believed God. They declared a fast, and all of them, from the greatest to the least, put on sackcloth.
>
> When the news reached the king of Nineveh, he rose from his throne, took off his royal robes, covered himself with sackcloth and sat down in the dust. (Jonah 3:4–6 NIV)

The king decreed a citywide fast during which all the men in Nineveh were to turn from their wicked ways, repent of their sins, and seek the face of God.

That touched God's heart.

> When God saw what they did and how they turned from their evil ways, he had compassion and did not bring upon them the destruction he had threatened. (Jonah 3:10 NIV)

Because Jonah's heart was not with the people there, he became angry when the nation of Nineveh saw their wickedness, repented, and turned to God. Scripture tells us that Jonah was greatly displeased and angry.

> But Jonah was greatly displeased and became angry. (Jonah 4:1 NIV)

The very next verse tells us that Jonah told the Lord that this was the very thing he was trying to avoid by running away to Tarsha, Now I don't know about you, but I read this scripture with tongue in cheek. How could Jonah have been so bold, arrogant, and full of himself that He would tell God who could repent of their sins, be saved, and start living their lives for God and who could not. I mean, really? What was Jonah thinking? God is all powerful. So powerful that He could have sucked the air out of Jonah's lungs!

And yet have we all not done the same thing with people we knew were living wicked lives? God pricks their hearts, bleeds out all the wickedness, and fills them with His love and the Holy Spirit, exactly what we have been praying for. But then when this happens, we feel some spiritual resentment (if I may call it that) because we have been serving God all these years while they have been serving only themselves.

We all have a Nineveh in our lives. And we all have a bit of Jonah as well. We all have someone whom the Lord asked us to either witness or mentor to. And when we did so, God blessed their socks off. In fact, God's blessings were so great that it caused us —caused me—to ask if this person truly deserved so many blessings. God gives to each one of us as He pleases. And God is no respecter of men. And even though we all have had a Nineveh and had been someone's Jonah, ultimately it is God who does the saving.

But there is another story to this scripture. A story of a father's love. The heavenly Father's. Jonah was disobedient to God, so God put Jonah in time-out. Jonah then pleaded to God to let be out. Jonah was in essence saying "I'm sorry, Daddy. I won't do it again!" We all have heard such pleadings from our children. God could have just ignored Jonah's pleading, but He responded to Jonah's prayer with love. And again, when Jonah had a temper tantrum with God because of Nineveh's repenting, God scolded Jonah. He then followed it up with the same type and amount of mercy and love that He showed Nineveh.

God will rebuke us if we need it and might put us in time-out if we need it. God rebukes those He loves. His children. But when we repent for our actions, He forgives us and showers us with His love and mercy. Every time.

But Words Will Deeply Harm Me

Remember the saying we said as children, "Sticks and stones may break my bones, but words will never harm me"? As an attempt to soothe their hurt feelings, I taught this to my children. However, this saying is not quite true. According to scripture, the saying really should be, "Sticks and stones can break my bones and words can deeply harm me."

God's Word tells us that though they are small, our tongues can control our actions. They can set our course. They can create wildfires of iniquity so great the fire defiles the entire body.

> Indeed, we put bits in horses' mouths that they may obey us, and we turn their whole body. Look also at ships; although they are so large and are driven by fierce winds, they are turned by a very small rudder wherever the pilot desires. Even so the tongue is a little member and boasts great things. See how great a forest little fire kindles! And the tongue is a fire, a world of iniquity. The tongue is so set among our members that it defiles the whole body, and sets on fire the course of nature; and it is set on fire by hell. (James 3:3–6 NKJV)

Words can be sign of our heart's condition. What comes out of the mouth comes from the heart. And sometimes those things are not what they should be. Jesus Himself, taught us so.

> "But those things which proceed out of the mouth come from the heart, and they defile a man. For out of the heart proceed evil thoughts, murders, adulteries, fornications, thefts, false witness, blasphemies." (Matthew 15:18–19 NKJV)

Once the tongue delivers harmful words, they are out in the open forever. Floating around in space. Never to be put back in your mouth again. Have you ever tried to unsay something you have said? The more you try to unsay it, the more you seem to say it!

Words that are mishandled are dangerous weapons. Yes, sticks and stones may very well break our bones, but words can harm us as well. They cut us deep inside. They damage our hearts, our souls, and even possibly our Christian walk. Unlike broken bones that heal, we may never fully heal from the injury of hurtful words.

So, before we use our words as swords cutting others down, we need to take a moment and remember the power that is in our tongues. We need to remember the wounds that our powerful sword may inflict. We need to think about the damage that our words may cause. To remember what God has told us about our tongues.

> Death and life are in the power of the tongue, and those who love it will eat its fruit. (Proverbs 18:21 NKJV)

Yes, our words, when used harmfully could cause death! Ouch!

Please allow me to state that I am not throwing stones here. But I am talking from my own personal experience. As you can see the Lord has given me the gift of gab. And if I am not careful, Satan will most assuredly use my gift as the gift of jab!

And that is not all. Let us look at how James 3 describes our tongues.

1. *Likes to brag.*
2. *And likes to spread rumors like wildfire.* Even so the tongue is a little member and boasts great things. See how great a forest a little fire kindle! (James 3:5 NKJV).
3. *Causes one to live a life of hellish fire.* And the tongue is a fire, a world of iniquity. The tongue is so set among our members that it defiles the whole body, and sets on fire the course of nature; and it is set on fire by hell (James 3:6 NKJV).
4. *Can be extremely toxic.* For every kind of beast and bird, of reptile and creature of the sea, is tamed and has been tamed by humankind. But no man can tame the tongue. It is an unruly evil, full of deadly poison (James 3:7–8 NKJV).
5. *Can be forked like that of a serpent's. For we use our tongues to not only condemn our fellow Christian but to praise our Lord.* With it we bless our God and Father, and with it we curse men, who have been made in the similitude of God. Out of the same mouth proceed blessing and cursing. My brethren, these things ought not to be so. Does a spring send forth

fresh water and bitter from the same opening? Can a fig tree, my brethren, bear olives, or a grapevine bear figs? Thus no spring yields both salt water and fresh (James 3:9–12 NKJV).

6. *It is restless and deadly. We all like to talk. And sometimes we talk too much. And when we do, what we say cuts someone like a butcher's knife. Therefore, the Lord has warned us that it is better to be quiet and thought a fool that to open our mouths and prove it.* Even a fool is counted wise when he holds his peace; when he shuts his lips, he is considered perceptive. (Proverbs 17:28 NJKV)

I'm Just One Person

Have you ever heard someone say, "What difference can I make? I'm just one person!" In the human world, this is a justifiable question, but let us take a look at what God said about what just one person could do.

Moses

Moses was just one man who freed an entire nation. Exodus tells us of a Jewish man who was raised in Pharaoh's palace as if he had been born into Pharaoh's family. Oddly enough, when Pharaoh's daughter needed someone to nurse the man when he was an infant, it was the man's Hebrew mother who was chosen for the task. Once the infant was a man, God used him to free the Hebrews from captivity by the Egyptians and lead them through the desert to a land God had promised them. On the way, God also gave His nation their Ten Commandments through the man of Moses.

First God told Moses how to prepare the people for His visit with Him.

> And the LORD said to Moses, "Behold, I come to you in the thick cloud, that the people may hear when I speak with you, and believe you forever." So Moses told the words of the people to the LORD.
>
> Then the LORD said to Moses, "Go to the people and consecrate them to day and

tomorrow, and let them wash their clothes. And let them be ready for the third day. For on the third day the LORD will come down upon Mount Sinai in the sight of all the people." (Exodus 19:10-11 NKJV)

And Moses prepared the people for the coming of the Lord, just as he had been instructed.

> So Moses went down from the mountain to the people and sanctified the people, and they washed their clothes. And he said to the people, "Be ready for the third day; do not come near your wives."

> Then it came to pass on the third day, in the morning, that there were thunderings and lightnings, and a thick cloud on the mountain; and the sound of the trumpet was very loud, so that all the people who were in the camp trembled. And Moses brought the people out of the camp to meet with God, and they stood at the foot of the mountain. Exodus 19:14–17 NKJV)

Then as we see in Chapter 20, the Lord gave Moses the Ten Commandments.

David

David, the youngest son of Jesse, was just one man—a boy—who rid Israel of a giant.

And Saul said to David, "You are not able to go against this Philistine to fight with him; for you are youth, and he a man of war from his you." (1 Samuel 17:33 NKJV)

David was not big enough to wear the armor of a solider, but he slew a giant. Not just any giant. A giant who was nine feet tall and very strong. Whose coat of armor weighed 125 pounds. A giant named Goliath, a Philistine who taunted the Israelites asking them why they even bothered to come to the line of battle if they were not going to fight him. David took down this giant with only a slingshot.

Then David said to the Philistine, "You come to me with a sword, with a spear, and with a javelin. But I come to you in the name of the Lord of hosts, the God of the armies of Israel, whom you have defied. This day the Lord will deliver you into my hand, and I will strike you and take your head from you. And this day I will give the carcasses of the camp of the Philistines to the birds of the air and the wild beasts of the earth, that all the earth may know that there is a God in Israel. Then all this assembly shall know that the Lord does not save with sword and spear; for the battle is the Lord's, and He will give you into our hands." (1 Samuel 17:45–47 NKJV)

Peter

Peter was just one man who led thousands of people to the Lord at one time. When I think of Peter, I think of a man who might have been very rugged and physically strong. A man who tended to jump into action before engaging his brain. Peter is best remembered for denying Jesus three times before the rooster crowed a few hours after promising Jesus that he would lay down his life for Him.

Even with all his shortcomings, Peter was the disciple who took on a crowd of people who were hurling accusations and led three thousand to Christ and then baptized them. All at once! Acts tell us that Peter spoke publicly after receiving the Holy Spirit.

> "Therefore let all the house of Israel know assuredly that God has made this Jesus, whom you crucified, both Lord and Christ."

> Now when they heard this, they were cut to the heart, and said to Peter and the rest of the apostles, "Men and brethren, what shall we do?"

> Then Peter said to them, "Repent, and let every one of you be baptized in the name of Jesus Christ for the remission of sins; and you shall receive the gift of the Holy Spirit. For the promise is to you and to your children, and to all who are afar off, as many as the Lord our God will call."

> And with many other words he testified and exhorted them, saying, "Be saved from this perverse generation."

Then those who gladly received his word were baptized; and that day about three thousand souls were added to them. (Acts 2:36–41 NKJV)

Adam

Adam was just one man who made one bad decision that will affect all humankind until Jesus comes again.

Then the LORD God commanded the man, saying, "Of every tree of the garden you may freely eat; but of the tree of the knowledge of good and evil you shall not eat, for in the day that you eat of it you shall surely die." (Genesis 2:16–17 NKJV)

Adam was commanded by God not to eat of the fruit of the Tree of the Knowledge of Good and Evil, but at the beckoning of Eve, he did. This one act has caused woman to be cursed with painful childbirth and man with the hardship of working for food. Adam's one bad decision is the reason we have such things as thorns and thistles.

Now the serpent was more cunning than any beast of the field which the LORD God had made. And he said to the woman, "Has God indeed said, 'You shall not eat of every tree of the garden'?"

And the woman said to the serpent, "We may eat of the fruit of the trees of the garden; but of the fruit of the tree which is in the midst of the garden, God has said, 'You shall not eat it, nor shall you touch it, lest you die.'"

Then the serpent said to the woman "You will not surely die. For God knows that in the day you eat of it your eyes will be opened, and you will be like God, knowing good and evil."

So when the woman saw that the tree was good for food, that it was pleasant to the eyes, and a tree desirable to make one wise, she took of its fruit and ate. She also gave to her husband with her, and he ate. (Genesis 3:1–6 NKJV)

Adam's one bad decision to sin created the need for the grain and blood sacrifices we read about in Leviticus. Adam's sin made sacrifices necessary. The act of just one man brought sin into the world and created a need for atonement through blood sacrifices. For unless there is a blood sacrifice, there cannot be remission of sin.

And according to the law almost all things are purified with blood, and without shedding of blood there is no remission. (Hebrews 9:22 NKJV)

So, my fellow Christian, you *can* make a difference - even if you are just one person.

Jeremiah 2:13

"My people have committed two sins: They have forsaken me, the spring of living water, and have dug their own cisterns, broken cisterns that cannot hold water." (Jeremiah 2:13 NIV)

When you are digging your own cistern, you are living life in your own strength, not in God's strength. Your cistern cannot hold God's promises because it will be full of holes, which will allow God's promises to leak out.

And so, it is when you try to live your way rather than God's way. When you live according to the world's standards, your life will be like a cistern which is full of holes. A cistern that cannot hold water. The Living Water. Your life will be void of God's Word, God's ways and God's promises.

But what are the promises that we would like to not leak out of our cisterns?

1. God promised us water from the wells of salvation.

   Surely God is my salvation; I will trust and not be afraid. The LORD, the LORD is my strength and my song; he has become my salvation. With joy you will draw water from the wells of salvation. (Isaiah 12:2–3 NIV)

2. God promised to pour out His Spirit, and blessings on us and our families.

For I will pour water on the thirsty land, and streams on the dry ground; I will pour out my Spirit on your offspring, and my blessing on your descendants. (Isaiah 44:3–4 NIV)

3. God promised us the Holy Spirit.

On the last and greatest day of the Feast, Jesus stood and said in a loud voice, "If anyone is thirsty, let him come to me and drink. Whoever believes in me, as the Scripture has said, streams of living water will flow from within him." By this he meant the Spirit, whom those who believed in him were later to receive. Up to that time the Spirit had not been given, since Jesus had not yet been glorified. (John 7:37–39 NIV)

4. God promised us anyone who drinks of this living water will have eternal life.

Jesus answered, "Everyone who drinks this water will be thirsty again, but whoever drinks the water I give him will never thirst. Indeed, the water I give him will become in him a spring of water welling up to eternal life." (John 4:13–14 NIV)

5. God promised us that we could live with Him.

I saw the Holy city, the new Jerusalem, coming down out of heaven from God, prepared as a bride beautifully dressed for her husband. And I heard a loud voice from the throne saying, "Now the dwelling of God is with men, and he will live with them." (Revelation 21:2–3 NIV)

6. God promised us that we would be His people and He would be our God.

'They will be his people, and God himself will be with them and be their God.' (Revelation 21:3 NIV)

7. God promised that He would wipe our tears from our eyes and that we would no longer deal with pain and death.

'He will wipe every tear from their eyes. There will be not more death or mourning or crying or pain, for the old order of things has passed away.' (Revelation 21:4 NIV)

8. God promised that we can freely drink from the spring of life.

He said to me: "It is done. I am the Alpha and the Omega, the Beginning and the End. To him who is thirsty I will give to drink without cost from the spring of the water of life." (Revelation 21:6–7 NIV)

What wonderful promises! I don't want a cistern with holes in it or a life that is not pleasing to God. A life lived in my own strength. A life relying on a broken cistern.

I would much rather have one that has been made in God's strength. One without holes. One that will hold God's promises. I do not want any of God's promises to leak out of my cistern.

David's Firstborn with Bathsheba

So David said to Nathan, "I have sinned against the LORD." And Nathan said to David, "The LORD also has put away your sin; you shall not die. However, because by this deed you have given great occasion to the enemies of the LORD to blaspheme, the child also who is born to you shall surely die," Then Nathan departed to his house.

And the LORD struck the child that Uriah's wife bore to David, and it became ill. David therefore pleaded with God for the child, and David fasted and went in and lay all night on the ground. So the elders of his house arose and went to him, to raise him up from the ground. But he would not, nor did he eat food with them.

Then on the seventh day it came to pass that the child died. And the servants of David were afraid to tell him that the child was dead. For they said, "Indeed, while the child was alive, we spoke to him, and he would not heed our voice. How can we tell him that the child is dead? He may do some harm!"

When David saw that his servants were whispering, David perceived that the child was dead. Therefore David said to his servants, "Is the child dead?" And they said, "He is dead."

So David arose from the ground, washed and anointed himself, and changed his clothes; and he went into the house of the LORD and worshiped. Then he went to his own house; and when he requested, they set food before him, and he ate.

Then his servants said to him, "What is this that you have done? You fasted and wept for the child while he was alive, but when the child died, you arose and ate food."

And he said, "While the child was alive, I fasted and wept; for I said, 'Who can tell whether the LORD will be gracious to me, that the child may live?' But now he is dead; why should I fast? Can I bring him back again? I shall go to him, but he shall not return to me." (2 Samuel 12:13–23 NKJV)

At first glance, this scripture might make it seem that David didn't care if the child lived or died. It might look as if David were saying, "Oh well. I have lots of other children." But I don't think this was the case. What I see in this passage is that David had sinned big-time. Not that any sin is any greater than another; in God's eyes, a sin is a sin. But, David had slept with someone else's wife and when she became pregnant he had her husband killed to cover up what he had done. That is a lesson of how sin multiplies. How once you have unconfessed and unrepented sin, you must continue sinning to keep the unconfessed and unrepented sin a secret.

Nathan, as a good friend, pointed out David's sin. God's Word tell us that we are to do the same. In face we are told that if we bring back someone who has strayed, we have saved his life.

> Brethren, if anyone among you wanders from the truth, and someone turns him back, let him know that he who turns a sinner from the error of his way will save a soul from death and cover a multitude of sins. (James 5:19–20 NKJV)

And that it is better to rebuke those we love than to hide the fact that we love them.

> Open rebuke is better than love carefully concealed. (Proverbs 27:5 NKJV)

For should we bring back anyone who has strayed from their Christian walk and do so in love we cover a multitude of sins. And boy, did David have a multitude of sins in his life at that moment.

David fasted, wept, and laid on the ground for seven days hoping God would change His mind and allow the child to live. David was asking, no he was begging God with his body, heart, mind, and soul to let his child live. David was giving it all he had. After all, he had fathered this child with a woman he loved. A woman he had killed for. This child was Bathsheba's firstborn son. A son who had been conceived in a sinful union. David's affair with

Bathsheba, a married woman. But David's request was denied. And the child died.

At times, our prayer requests are for things we should not have or do. Times when our heavenly Father will not allow us to have or to do the very things we are asking for in our prayer request. And it is not pleasant when this happens. When God says "no" to our request.

Sometimes I have poor-me pity parties when I hear God's no. Why, I have even been known to pout and to act like a spoiled child when I hear that answer. And yet Scripture does not tell us that David was angry with God. Or that he had a pity party. Or pouted. Or even rolled his eyes. What we do see in David's actions is an acceptance of God's will. David accepted God's "no" answer. He accepted God's will. He did not argue or try to bargain with Him.

No. What we see is David fully repenting of his sin with Bathsheba. David got up off the floor. And since he had not washed for seven days, he was dirty – unclean. So, he washed, anointed himself and changed clothes. Then David went into the house of the LORD and worshipped. And then he ate.

What a wonderful example of salvation. First there is repentance. Then there was the cleansing, and the anointing. Afterwards David removed his old clothing— his old ways—and put on new clothes for a new day. A new creation.

He then went to the temple to worship God. I believe that this was not only an act of repentance for his sin but was also an act of acceptance of God's answer to his prayers. An act of faith that God would forgive him. David was closing the door to the painful experience that he had just had. For David really loved Bathsheba, and the loss of their son would be very painful. David had learned from painful experiences of his past just where his strength came from and who he could turn to - God. David knew that only God was his strength - his refuge - his strong tower. So, David went to the temple where God was to renew his strength.

Only then, after he had spent time with God, did David eat. Remember David had been fasting for seven days. Even though he was assuredly extremely hungry, David worshipped before he ate. David knew his spiritual food was more important that his physical food.

David knew that he had messed up with Bathsheba. And he knew that God knew it. Willingly he accepted God's consequences for his actions. For his sins. David was being a living testimony to others of how a godly man behaves when he walks with God. How a godly man accepts God's answers to his prayers no matter what the answer is.

David was a living testimony to his servants. For they were perplexed and asked him, "Why are you acting this way?" They had been watching to see how he would handle the loss of his son. To see if he would accept God's "no". Just how would David act when God did not heal his son. And what did they see? A man who obediently accepted God's will for his life. No matter how painful the obedience is.

Wow! May I gently ask you a question. How are you handling the consequences for your sin? What do you do when God says no to you? Are you following David's example of a godly man's walk? Or is your tendency more towards temper tantrums and the rolling of eyes? (If I were to perfectly honest, I sometimes tilt to the temper tantrums. Arg.)

Remember, my fellow Christian, you're being watched. Just as David's servants watched him to see how he would handle God's answer, you have others who are watching you. Who are watching just how you handle the "no" answers given to you.

There is another lesson we can learn from this passage. In 2 Samuel 12:15, Bathsheba was referred to as Uriah's wife.

> Then Nathan departed to his house. And the LORD struck the child that Uriah's wife bore to David, and it became ill. (2 Samuel 12:15 NKJV)

But then, after David had accepted God's will and had repented for his sinful ways, we see in 2 Samuel 12:24 that Bathsheba was then called David's wife and that the Lord allowed Bathsheba to give David another son. A son who was not conceived in an adulterous union. A son who is known for asking the Lord for wisdom, Solomon.

> Then David comforted Bathsheba his wife, and went in to her and lay with her. So she bore a son, and he called his name Solomon. Now the LORD Love him. (2 Samuel 12:24 NKJV)

Only after David had accepted God's will, repented for his sins, and had worshipped Him did the Lord bless David by call Bathsheba his wife. And allowed her to bless him with a son. Not before. Not while David was begging. But after David had honestly repented of his sin.

Birthrights

> Now Jacob cooked a stew; and Esau came
> in from the field, and he was weary. And
> Esau said to Jacob, "Please feed me with that
> same red stew, for I am weary." Therefore his
> name was called Edom.
>
> But Jacob said, "Sell me your birthright as of
> this day." And Esau said, "Look, I am about
> to die; so what is this birthright to me?"
>
> Then Jacob said, "Swear to me as of this day."
> So he swore to him, and sold his birthright
> to Jacob. (Genesis 25:29–33 NKJV)

Is this not what those who do not know about their
birthrights given to them through the blood of Jesus, say?
Like Esau, they will quickly sell their birthrights for a bowl
of stew. Maybe Esau had no knowledge of or just did not
care about his birthright. About how valuable it was. Either
way, Esau saw this offer of food paid for with a birthright
that he though was worthless, as a good idea. A win-win.
For in the words of Esau, "Look, I am about to die; so what
is this birthright to me?"

And so, it is with those who are without salvation. For
without Jesus as their personal Savior they cannot know
how valuable their birthright through Jesus really is. Nor
can they know the knowledge of God, as their heavenly
Father. For you must know Jesus as your Savior before you
can know God. Jesus Himself told us so. Jesus told us that

those who know Him would know the Father because He and the Father are one. (John 10:30 NKJV)

Those who have not accepted God's gift of salvation have no knowledge of what they are giving up in exchange for a bowl of stew. They have not received their spiritual blessings from the heavenly Father. They have not tasted God's sweetness. Felt His awesome love and mercy. For they have not been washed in Jesus's blood and have not received the Holy Spirit. Until they do so, they cannot know how sweet and special and powerful their birthright through the blood of Jesus really is. They all too quickly and too willingly give away their birthright for the desires of the flesh. Just as Esau did.

If Jacob had treated his brother as Jesus taught us to treat our Christian brothers, he would have served Esau the stew just because Esau was hungry. There would have been no other reason. No other motive. No strings attached. And we would be reading something like:

"Jacob, what great smelling stew! I'm famished!"

"Sit down, Esau, and I'll serve you a great big bowl of it. Enjoy, my brother!"

But he didn't do that. Instead, he manipulated Esau into giving up something he wanted from Esau. Jacob treated Esau in a harsh and deceptive manner. How often have you seen this same scene in today's world? From adults and children alike. Neighbors with neighbors. Coworkers with coworkers. Even churchgoers with churchgoers.

Without Jesus as their personal Savior, people will continue to fall prey to the Jacobs of the world. Without Jesus as their personal Savior, they will continue to be manipulative as Jacob was. And sadly enough, they will continue to act as Esau did.

But the most tragic part of this story is, people who are without Jesus as their personal Savior are people who will sell, trade, or give away their birthrights for something they may want. Something they may think they need. They are the people who are most likely to trade off their souls, if you will, for fleshly desires. And they will do so again and again. Until the day arrives when they must face the consequences of their choices – eternity without God. Ouch!

O Ye of Little Faith

On many occasions, Jesus called His disciples, "O ye of little faith." They must have feared frequently, for Jesus had to say this very same thing repeatedly only in different ways. Makes one wonder, did His disciples not get it? Jesus is stranding right there with them and yet He must remind them not to fear.

And yet we tend to be just like the disciples. Or at least I tend to. I will run around saying such things as, "Jesus does not have to call me 'O ye of little faith'! No sirree! Not this follower! No way! Jesus has to be talking to someone else. I'm not the 'O ye of little faith' follower. I am the 'O ye of big faith'! For my faith is the kind that can move mountains, even the Swiss Alps, with just one hand! Yeppers! That's me! Ask me and I'll tell you just how much faith I have!"

But then here it comes. Boom – life! Finances are tight. It's one of those "just gonna squeak by" months. And oh man! My horse just ripped her leg wide open. Calling the vet is not just an option - it's a necessity.

So out he comes. He starts to mend my horse. And he doctors and doctors and doctors some more. As he tends to the medical needs of my horse, I see the $$$ adding up. Special tape for bandaging. Antibiotics for infection. Medication for pain. Salve for the wound. IV solution to flush the wound. He instructs me on how and when to administer each one. I can see his mouth moving but all I hear is *Ca-ching!* as my mental cash register starts ringing up my bill.

And then it arrives. The time to pay the doctor. He tells

me he won't cash my check until the following Monday. So I now have a week to do - what? Worry? Pray? Rob a bank?

My vet is now resting under a shade tree punching the keys on his laptop. With each finger stroke I own him more money. How ironic that the same hands that had just skillfully bandaged my wounded horse are draining my checking account. I go inside for my checkbook, and I see that the bank statement has come it. *Maybe? Could it be that there's enough money in my account to cover this unexpected expense?*

Swallowing hard I go outside with my checkbook in hand. Without any knowledge of my inner financial turmoil, my vet hands me the bill. And with a heightened amount of anxiety, I reach out, accept the bill, and look at the total amount due. *But wait. There must be something wrong. How much is that total due?*

Not believing the total amount due on the bill, I repeat it back to him. And he affirms the amount with a gentle smile. *Really? Wow! Whew! Thank you, Lord! I can cover this!*

But wait a moment. Isn't there something wrong with this story? Something like the absence of prayer? Why didn't I go to the Lord in prayer before I started worrying? Where was my faith when I saw that my horse had been injured? Why didn't I ask God to help me instead of worrying?

Had I forgotten that I was a Christian with access to God? Had I forgotten that I am the not the 'O ye of little faith' Christian but the 'heaping big faith' Christian? And then it hit me – I had acted just like Jesus's disciples did.

Even Christians with heaping big faith can fall down while walking their Christian walk. They can and will sometimes fail to go to God first before they turn to other things. This is why Jesus told us repeatedly not to fear and not to worry. Jesus told us that He knew how to care for those who belonged to Him. And that He would.

I was so sure of my Christianity in my own strength that I forgot where I got that strength from. I forgot to go to Jesus first and then tend to my problem. I forgot what Jesus told me ... not to fear or to worry.

> But He said to them, "Why are you fearful,
> O you of little faith?" Then He arose and
> rebuked the winds and the sea, and there
> was a great calm. (Matthew 8:26 NKJV)

I'd been so busy trying to do this in my own strength that I forgot Jesus was right there waiting to take my worries from me. I was so taken in by my circumstances that I forgot to pray. *Oops!*

Oh! That Book of Job!

How many of us avoid reading the book of Job? There was a time when God wanted me to read that book. *Arggh!* And of course, I, in all my humanly wisdom questioned God. *Are you sure, God? Now? When I'm going through one of the greatest hardships of my life you want me to read a book filled with sorrow? Can I not read the book of Psalms? My life's been stressful lately and the Psalms are soothing, so comforting. You want your children to be soothed and comforted, right?*

So, without waiting for an answer from the Lord, I, once again in my humanly wisdom, started reading Psalms.

God will have His way in our lives even when we rebel, and He did so in mine. That very day, one of my favorite radio preachers that I listen to spoke on Job. And then on my way to work, another favorite preacher also taught out? Yes, you guess it. Job.

But I was still asking, *Why Lord? Why Job? Why at this time of my life must I read a book filled with loss and sorrow? Lord please, do You not remember how depressing that book can be?*

Now I must put in a disclaimer by stating that I do not always have such behavior with God. And the few times that I have, He was patient with me and guided me to where He wants me to be. And such was the case here. Even though I was rebellious with God, He was faithful to me. He allowed me to hear from not one but two of my most favorite preachers teaching from the Book of Job. Since I did not go to the Scriptures, He wanted me to read, He brought them to me!

God's actions prompted me to say, "Thank you, Lord,

so much for your mercy and your love." And to pick up my Bible and to turned to Job – and to read it.

And – I did. Most of it. Not all of it. For I found some of it difficult. Sad. Reading about how Job suffered such loss when he had not done anything to deserve it broke my heart. The suffering of those who bring suffering on themselves is sad, but the suffering of an innocent victim is heartbreaking. And innocent Job was. For he was blameless and upright; he feared God and shunned evil.

> In the land of Uz there lived a man whose name was Job. This man was blameless and upright; he feared God and shunned evil. (Job 1:1 NIV)

Reading about Job enduring all those losses touched a chord of sadness in my heart. I too have tasted the bitterness of loss and defeat. The loss of material belongings - of a business - of income - family - and even my church. For the past few years it seems that my only purpose in life, was to endure another loss. And there I was reading about a man who was also acquainted with loss. In fact, very much the same loss. Only Job's were within hours, while mine took months.

God wanted to show me something. In Job 3, Job was stressed to the point of cursing the day he had been born. His suffering had pushed him to the point of suicide. He lamented the very day he was born.

Job was at a point where he needed to choose to live and to trust that God would help him through his trials. And in spite of all his misery and agony, the persistent begging of his wife, and the finger pointing of his friends, Job did just that. He decided to praise God even though life was extremely hard. Job made the critical choice to stay true to God. To continue trusting Him. And because of his choice, God restored all that Job had lost and then some.

Now, this is not a name-it-and-claim-it-lesson. This is a lesson about trusting God. While at a crossroads, Job chose to be faithful to God and to trust that God knew what He was doing. And because of his faithfulness to God, God rewarded Job greatly.

The lessons we can learn from Job are:

1. God rewards those who trust in Him.
2. God rewards those who wait on Him.
3. God is faithful to His children and rewards those who are faithful to Him.
4. God is very generous with His rewards.

Are you in a spot where you feel as though your life is chaotic and out of control? Are you feeling trapped by the circumstances in your life? May I suggest reading the book of Job. Start with chapter 1 and read until you realize that your life is no different from that of others. Read until you see that others have endured the same circumstances you are now enduring. Read until you realize that there is an end to your present circumstances and that God will reward you once you have endured should you stay faithful to Him. Feeling better? I thought you would.

Are You?

Disgusted with today's adulterous ways? Tired of those who tell you that homosexuality is just another lifestyle? That those who disagree are homophobes?

Weary of being shown what love is according to worldly standards? Concerned about our young people who have been deceived and just live together without marriage? Do you feel for the children of such unions as they are reared in the instability of these arrangements?

Want to see an end to abortions? At least the ones that are not for medical purposes?

Wanting for good to mean good and for bad to mean bad? For there to be an unblurred division between the two?

Longing for the days of fewer killings? For days when it was safe to go to malls? To congregate? The days when schools were safe? For the days when guns were for hunting game, not innocent people? And certainly not innocent children?

Tired of hateful, hideous crimes? Crimes that are beyond imagination? Crimes that appear to be bolder, more frequent, and more deadly.

Yearning for the good ol' days when men were kind to each other? The days when human life was valued? Days when it was common to help those who were in need often without others knowing? Times when it seemed as though people's hearts were softer and more open?

Remember the times when you could go to your neighbors without locking your door? When friends could be trusted with your thoughts and your secrets? Times when you knew that should you lend something, it would be looked after until it was returned? Times when promises were kept? When trust was easy?

Getting weary of being told that you have to be a good Christian and to endure it—whatever it happens to be—by those who confess not to be Christians? That unless you do so, you are not being tolerant? Isn't it strange that we Christians must be tolerant of their beliefs and lifestyles, but they do not have to be tolerant of ours?

Sick of hearing people use the Lord's name in vain and having to endure their insults when you ask others not to use your Lord's name in disrespectful ways? Tired of being told that you cannot say, pray, or even whisper the name Jesus Christ in public if used in a worshipful way?

Feeling a bit rejected by those who get in your face because you share the gospel? Rejected because you do not live as the world does? Rejected because you live by standards given to you from the Father?

Tired of the world's lies and the world believing them?

Want things to change? Then pray. Pray for all these things and for those who are doing them. Ask the Lord to give you the strength to continue living in a manner that pleases Him. To help you endure. In doing so, you will be showing them who Jesus really is through your actions.

Then do as Jesus commanded you to do.

> And Jesus came and spoke to them, saying, "All authority has been given to Me in heaven and on earth. Go therefore and make disciples of all the nations, baptizing them in the name of the Father and of the Son and of the Holy Spirit, teaching them

to observe all things that I have commanded you; and lo, I am with you always, even to the end of the age." Amen. (Matthew 28:18–20 NKJV)

Go out into the world and tell them about Jesus. Tell everyone you see. Tell them how Jesus can change their lives. Tell them of His power over addictions, and strongholds. Tell them of His love for them. And how He gave the greatest of sacrifices for them. He gave His life.

And tell everyone! Your neighbor. Your doctor. Your banker. The grocery cashier. Your accountant. Your attorney. Your aunt. Your uncle. Everyone!

Tell the man who takes your money at the gas station. The mailman. The maintenance man. The repair man. The teller at your bank. And as in my case, tell your vet, your feed man, your farrier. You might even tell the homeless man standing there with his sign. Or those who are sitting in a doctor's waiting room with you. Maybe even, those who are standing in line next to you. But tell. Tell everyone.

When you do, one of two things will happen. Those you talk to may realize that Jesus is the Messiah, that He is their way to heaven, and accept Him as their personal Savior, their sacrificial sin Lamb. When they do, they will receive the Holy Spirit, which will allow them to start living new lives directed by the Holy Spirit. The Holy Spirit will help them lose any desire to live in worldly ways and to replace it with the desire to live in a righteous way.

They will develop a hunger for living as God wants them to live, which means they will no longer want to have relationships that are an abomination to God. They will no longer use God's name as a cuss word but will use it with the holy reverence it deserves. These people will no longer stomach abortions, lies, adultery, and other such ways of the world. They will begin walking the same Christian path that you are on and will have the same Christian values you have.

Or Jesus will return to the earth to gather His church. Once all the world has heard the gospel and has had a chance to accept Him as their personal Savior, Jesus is coming back for us. Jesus told us that once the gospel was preached to the world—to all the nations, to all the mailmen, the grocery workers, doctors, gas station attendants, neighbors, family members—to all, the end will come. Remember what Jesus told us?

> "And this gospel of the kingdom will be preached in all the world as a witness to all nations, and then the end will come." (Matthew 24:14 NKJV)

By spreading the gospel, either souls will be saved, or the rapture will come. And this, for Christians, is a win-win!

Love Is Powerful

> But when the Pharisees heard that He had silenced the Sadducees, they gathered together; then one of them, a lawyer, asked Him a question, testing Him, and saying, "Teacher, which is the great commandment in the law?"
>
> Jesus said to him, "You shall love the LORD your God with all your heart, with all your soul, and with all you mind. This is the first and great commandment. And the second is like it: 'You shall love your neighbor as yourself.'" (Matthew 22:34–39 NKJV)

Jesus told the Pharisees that the greatest commandment was to love the Lord, their God, with all their hearts, minds, and souls. He told them that there was a second commandment: Love their neighbors as themselves. For love is that powerful.

I know a woman who wanted to learn how to ride horses and bought a skinny, broken-down horse that came with lots of bad behavior. The horse would back her ears (a sign of aggression) when anyone would come near her. She would refuse to accept a bit and putting a halter on her was so difficult that once we were able to get one on, we left it on.

But this woman fell in love with this horse. She just had to have that badly behaved mount. She was determined to love this horse despite the horse's rude and at times dangerous behavior.

Several months later when I visited her, I could not believe my eyes. The horse who once behaved badly now looked much younger and healthier. The once broken-down horse was now walking with a spring in her step. The look in the horse's eye was not that of rebellion but of contentment and cooperation. And the horse was behaving in a very nice manner. You could put a halter on her without a fight. She was not only accepting the bridle willingly but was actually looking for the bit. And - the horse appeared to be smiling! Yes – smiling! What a dramatic change. She definitely was not the same horse of a few months earlier.

What changed this horse? What created such willing obedience? Why did this horse now have a spring in her step? And what put that smile on her face?

Love. Real, sincere, patient love. This woman cared for this horse, and she allowed her love for this horse to show. The woman groomed her horse, cared for her needs, and showered her with hugs and kisses. Yes, you can hug and kiss a horse. She really loved this horse, and the horse responded to her love.

Need another example? I have a horse named Molly. She came to me with issues of mistrust. She showed signs of having been used hard by humans. It was as if she had decided not to trust humans anymore. Unlike most horses that do not trust humans, Molly did not show bad behavior. She was just untrusting. She would do what you asked of her but with fear.

Molly has been treated with lots of love, lots of honesty and with even more love and honesty. If I ask her to do something for which she gets a treat, then there is a treat when she is done. If she becomes fearful, she isn't scolded; she is reassured and comforted. And loved.

Molly has responded to this type of treatment in such a way that she will now follow humans begging for a kind word, a rub and a hug. She comes to the fence and calls to me when I walk out of the house. Molly knowns that someone loves her - really loves her, and she has responded back with love.

The power of love is amazing. It can be a driving force that keeps us soft and kind to others. It is why we enjoy doing things for those who can't do them for themselves. It gives a defending parent great courage and strength. And it creates a lifelong bond between a husband and wife. It is our motivator for taking care of our neighbors. And it is important to God.

> And now abide faith, hope, love, these three; but the greatest of these is love. (1 Corinthians 13:13 NKJV)

Please think about this. If God thinks that love is the greatest, should not we? And if our love can effectively change behavior, think about what God's love can do. How it can change the hearts of man.

Jesus told us what God's love can do:

> "For God so loved the world that He gave His only begotten Son, that whoever believes in Him should not perish but have everlasting life. For God did not send His Son into the world to condemn the world, but that the world through Him might be saved." (John 3:16–17 NKJV)

And then - He demonstrated it.

Sin's Lure

In Luke 15:11–31 we find a story about two brothers working on a farm with their father. All seemed well until the youngest brother decided he wanted out. He wanted his father to give him his cut of his inheritance so he could go and live in another area and sow his wild oats. To which his father agreed.

With a pocketful of money and a desire to experience life's fleshly desires, the younger son left on his adventure. Can you picture him skipping down that dusty lane with a song in his heart and visions of happiness in his mind? How happy the younger brother must have been to be rid of his older brother, farm life, and his father's authority.

Perhaps the younger brother had heard stories of how other people live. How these people seem to be free from the boundaries created by moral living and his father. Or perhaps the younger brother had tired of the daily hard work that farm life requires or had become bored with it. Whatever the case the younger brother fell victim to the lure of sinful life.

Scripture tells us that once his money was gone, so were his friends. Scripture also tells us that the younger brother had to start feeding pigs so to feed himself. It was at this point – at the lowest point of his newly found life of freedom – that he came to his senses and went home.

When the younger brother arrived at his father's farm, he found that his father had been waiting for his return. Not just waiting- but watching *and* waiting.

He found that his father was not angry with him for leaving or for coming home broke and broken. No. Instead his father ran out to greet him compassionately with hugs and kisses.

The younger brother responded to such compassion, and acceptance with true remorse for his actions. True remorse for the type of life that he had been living. A life that was filled with sinful ways. And he told his father that he was not worthy of such acceptance and compassion, and he was no longer worthy of being his son.

This story could very well be a story of everyone who has accepted Jesus as their Savior and strayed from their walk with Him. This story shows us how sin can lure us from our intended walk. How sin can look good from a distance and be so ugly up close.

It is also a story of how they are accepted when they decide to come back into the fold of God's children. How they are greeted with love and acceptance. How they are truly restored and made who.

The festival in this story reminds me of the angels that rejoice and celebrate every time someone repents and accepts Jesus Christ as their Savior either for the first time or when they return straying.

In the words of Jesus:

> "I say to you that likewise there will be more joy in heaven over one sinner who repents than over ninety-nine just persons who need no repentance." (Luke 15:7 NKJV)

Who Has the Reins?

Horses are great animals. God has a special place in His heart for them. He spoke about them in the Bible, and Jesus and the armies in heaven will be riding a white horse.

> Now I saw heaven opened, and behold, a white horse. And He who sat on him was called Faithful and True, and in righteousness He judges and makes war. His eyes were like a flame of fire, and on His head were many crowns. He had a name written that no one knew except Himself. He was clothed with a robe dripped in blood, and His name is called The Word of God. And the armies in heaven, clothed in fine linen, white and clean, followed Him on white horses. (Revelation 19:11–14 NKJV)

Horses can teach us how to be good Christians. The primary form of behavior that we as riders ask from our horses is obedience. We tell our horses to turn this way or that. We tell them where to go and how fast to get there. We tell them when to stop and where to stand still. And we expect our horses to follow our lead without question. To be obedient.

Horses with more-advanced training are told which leg to lead off on when picking up a gait. We tell them how to hold their heads, when to bend their bodies and how long to do so. Andy6gt6, they are asked to do so without questioning the cues of their riders or the leadership of their handlers.

When they are obedient, things go well. Horse and rider appear to become as one. Like dancers executing an elegant waltz. Obedience is good.

But there are times when our horses are full of themselves and not obedient to their riders. It seems they cannot hear our commands or cannot understand them. Either way, they are not obeying them. Instead, they do what they want to do. They follow the lead of their willfulness and not the lead of their riders. This misbehavior almost always turns into disaster with either the rider or the horse being injured. And sometimes both. Disobedience is not good.

The primary behavior our Lord asks from us is obedience. When we are obedient, all things fall into place without disaster or injury. But when we become full of our own will and do as we want, things become chaotic. Just like our horses, we seem to lose the ability to hear our Master's voice. And we no longer follow His lead but ours instead. We run around without His guidance not knowing where to turn, where to go, or how fast to get there which always turns into disaster. And there will always be injuries.

We must stay in God's will. Listen to His voice. Follow His guidance. Turn when He says to turn. Go when He says to go. Run and then stop on His command. If we obey Him, He will guide us and make us steadfast and confident.

Let God have the reins of your life. He knows far better that you do, and He will guide you through whatever comes your way. He sees all. He knows all. He is the only one in control. Just as we love our horses, God loves us. Only God's love is thousands of times greater than we could imagine.

God has work for us to do. And He will equip us with the talents and abilities we need to perform His work. He will give us the opportunities and the provisions required. But we have to be obedient and willing. And we have to hand Him the reins of our lives.

Yes, it's scary to let go. To allow someone else, even God, to take the reins of our lives. Sometimes, it takes a lot of faith to allow God to have total control over everything in our lives. But I have a secret for you. God is in control over everything anyway. Even when we are holding the reins, God is still in control. We just sometimes forget.

Strangers in the World

Because we are a home church, Saturdays are the days my church worships. We meet every Saturday night to pray, sing, and worship Jesus Christ and our heavenly Father. Afterward, we feast on a wonderful sermon and a fellowship dinner. It is such a sweet time. I look forward to it every week.

Worshipping on Saturday leaves Sundays open for family time. So, one Sunday, my husband and I went to a local flea market. While walking around the market, I felt something foreign with my soul. As morning became noon and the crowd grew, I began to feel more and more uncomfortable. For I was now surrounded with people using foul language and talking crudely. I overheard bragging on just how much they could drink and still stand up. A man was talking about his gambling telling all how much he had won. However, despite his great winnings, he still showed signs of poverty. How sad.

Another man tried to convince me that he was the only person I could trust for advice on plants. He tried to convince me that all the other vendors selling plants in the market were just there to take my money. He told me that he was there to help me with my plants. And only help me with my plants. For a price.

The older the day grew, the more uncomfortable I became. By the time we had walked the entire market, I was so ready to leave. I just wanted to run to my truck, jump into it and flee.

Once in the safety of the cab, I quietly wondered if maybe I had experienced what Satan's camp was like. If perhaps what I had experienced was Satan flexing his muscles while trying to impress me with just how big, bold, and powerful he was. And how he could control people's actions.

The Lord told us that we would know people by their fruit. And from the actions of these people, they appeared not to be children of God, or not walking their Christian walk. Scripture tells us that God's children will show such fruits as love, joy, peace, forbearance, kindness, goodness, and faithfulness. Fruits of which I saw very little of. I did see an occasional kindness, but the other fruits were like - AWOL.

God's Word tells us that we are either His Children or Satan's. There is no in between. No gray area. No neutrality. No fence to sit on. We are God's children because we have accepted Jesus Christ as our savior and have been washed by His blood. Or - we are Satan's children by default. Period.

Could it be that what I really saw were souls crying out for help? Tormented souls who were trying anything they could to take away the fear? To medicate the pain. Souls who were under bondage and needed freedom but did not realize their bondage? Souls who didn't know they could go to Jesus for the freedom they needed. Souls who did not know that Jesus's blood is much more powerful than any bondage, any addition or anything else Satan could inflict them with?

Or perhaps they were souls who believed they were too dirty or too bad to go to Jesus. Who believed that no one, especially God and His Son Jesus, could love them because they are too bad or too dirty? Or too far gone. That they were perhaps - beyond help.

Lies. Lies. And more lies. All lies. Jesus told us that Satan is the father of lies. That his native language was lying. That any time Satan's lips are moving, he is lying. And yes, I do believe that Satan was talking to those people. Telling them lies. That they were not worthy of anything. That they were too gross, too foul, too far gone to go to someone like Jesus for help. Lies and more lies.

For, Satan talks to me. He gets on my shoulder and tries to tell me the same lies. That I am not good enough for Jesus. Who do I think I am trying to write for Jesus? Telling others about God and about the things of God? If he is bold enough to come after me, one who has the seal of God on her forehead, then those who do not carry God's mark are easy game.

Then an awful thought came to mind. Maybe these people do not know how to go to Jesus. Maybe they do not know that all they need to do is to call out to Jesus. To earnestly repent of their sin, ask Him for forgiveness, accept Jesus as their sacrificial sin Lamb and then they too can be one of God's children. If that's the case, I must hang my head and say, "Shame on us, church! Shame on me!"

Jesus told us to make disciples of all men. All men. Not some men, but all men. Now, I know that certain places can be extremely uncomfortable. And I know that sometimes people do and say things that are distasteful. That it may be a bit difficult to really enjoy being in the presence of those who are openly and willingly living in sin. But Jesus told us to make disciples and to baptize all men. Not just those who are only a little bad. Or just a little lost. But those who are really lost. Really bad. Yes, even those people. Remember? <u>ALL</u> men. No matter their present lifestyle.

> Then Jesus came to them and said, "All authority in heaven and on earth has been given to me. Therefore go and make disciples of all nations, baptizing them in the name of the Father and of the Son and of the Holy Spirit, and teaching them to obey everything I have commanded you. And surely I am with you always, to the very end of the age." (Matthew 28:18–20 NIV)

And They're Off!

Up early. No breakfast, blood tests today.

Just some coffee just to wake up. Quick shower. Quick prayer. Grab the outgoing mail. Check purse for phone. Out the door. Out the gate. And I'm off.

Outpatient lab for blood work. A visit to the ICU to say goodbye to a dear sister in Christ. Home to tend to business. Do a few household chores. Off to a doctor's appointment. Phone calls. Texts with others about the sister who had just passed. Pick up mother-in-law and off to another hospital to visit sister-in-law. More texts. More calls.

Visiting sister-in-law at hospital. Oh! It's 5:00 p.m., and praise team practice is at 6:30 in New Port Richey and am in Clearwater. Quick kisses. Gotta go! Back into the car. Out on the road going north as quickly as I can while staring at a long line of red brake lights.

Arggh! Big sigh. Rolling eyes.

More calls. More texts. (I am not driving.) Finally, I reach New Port Richey. Drop off mother-in-law at her home. A little voice is saying, "Check to see if there really is practice." And we all know who that little voice is, don't we? Sure enough ... no practice. Not calling to let me know was an oversight. Whew! Quick "thank You Lord" for the night off prayer.

Supper time comes. It's too late to cook. Pull up to a chicken fast-food place. I stand in a long line to place my order with a sweet-sounding young lady. When she tells me how much my order will cost, I gasp. Surely, she's made a mistake. I try to explain that there must be an error with the amount. She begins to argue with me because she doesn't make mistakes. *"Arggh"* Exhausted and drained from the day, I say to my husband in a small wee voice, "Honey, please take me home."

Arriving at our destination, my hubby and I struggle to walk into our home we are so hungry and exhausted. Eating in quiet, we hope that no one texts, comes over or calls. We feel spent, and we need to recharge. No TV. No radio. No conversation. Nothing. Just quietness and food.

As I reflect on my day, I think about losing have losing a dear friend. A woman who I deeply loved. How I held her mourning husband as he wept for his loss. How I tended to the needs of God's church. Helped a family member visit her hospitalized daughter. Attempted to put out a family fire. Had a meltdown in Clearwater's 5:00 p.m. traffic. And almost attended a cancelled practice.

Spent from the demands of the day, I whispered a small prayer, "Lord, I just can't do this anymore. I'm done. Drained. This Christian life is just way too hard. Too demanding. I'm too tired to continue. I can't do this on my own!"

But then God very lovingly and gently shows me something. Yes, this has been a hard day, one you may never want to repeat. God quietly reminded me that being a Christian does not exempt me from having bad days or give me a "Get Out of Stress Free" card. But - being a Christian *did mean* that I would have Him to help me through such days. That when I became tired, anxious, angry, overwhelmed, or sad, *I could go to Jesus* for help, *and* He would be there to help me - *every time.*

When those who do not live for God—those who do

not have a personal relationship with Jesus—have hard days, they usually try to medicate themselves with alcohol or drugs. They feel as though they have nothing else to turn to. And unless they have Jesus they may not.

Christians pray when they have hard days. They go to Jesus for help, for relief from the day's aches and pains, and for comfort. Christians have Jesus and God to go to when they need their batteries charged. They have Jesus and God as their refuge. In fact that is just the very thing Jesus told us to do.

> "Come to Me, all you who labor and are heavy laden, and I will give you rest. Take My yoke upon you and learn from Me, for I am gentle and lowly in heart, and you will find rest for your souls. My yoke is easy and My burden is light." (Matthew 11:28–30 NKJV)

Christians know they have the privilege of going to Jesus with their hurts. They fully understand that because Jesus loves them That He willingly laid His life down for them. That He died as the sacrificial sin Lamb that was needed to satisfy God's requirement of a blood sacrifice for sin.

And Christians understand that they too had a time when they would turn to alcohol or drugs as an attempt to soothing fried nerves. Or to escape the stress of a hard day. That is until they accepted Jesus as their Savior. And - now they have Him to turn to.

They also understand that by filling their minds and souls and emotions up with the things of God, they are actually being drawn closer to God. And the closer to God they get, the closer to Him they want to be. Strange how that happens.

And enduring such days is a reminder that we cannot do life in our own strength. No. We need to pick up Jesus's yoke and allow God to give us His strength.

The Just and the Unjust

Every morning God tells His sun to rise on both the unrighteous and the righteous – the good and the evil. He also allows rain to fall on both the righteous an the unrighteous – the good and the evil. He allows them to experience happy times and sad times. Rich times and poor times. Our Lord, Jesus Christ, has told us this:

> "You have heard that it was said, 'You shall love your neighbor and hate your enemy.' But I say to you, love your enemies, bless those who curse you, do good to those who hate you, and pray for those who spitefully use you and persecute you, that you may be sons of your Father in heaven; for He makes His sun rise on the evil and on the good, and sends rain on the just and on the unjust." (Matthew 5:43–45 NKJV)

After reading the above Scripture I have this question -why? Why will the Lord allow the unjust to experience the same joys and benefits of refreshing rain as the just do? Do not the just deserve to feel the coolness that comes with a gentle rain? Or the sweet smell of the flowers that are sustained by rain? After all, they are not only the just but they are righteous.

And what if the rain should come in the way of a storm? With torrential flooding, dangerous lightning, loud thunder, and blustery winds? Why would the Lord allow the just to experience the same torrential storms as the unjust? Do not the unjust deserve these storms? Have they not brought such storms on themselves by being unjust? By being unrighteous?

Are the righteous not the children of God? Have they not been sealed with the seal of God? Why must they endure the same trials as those who have the seal of God. Does God not love His children?

Of course, He does. It is because He loves us that He allows the unjust to enjoy the gentle rains and the just to experience the storms. He is waiting for the unjust, the unrighteous, to become just and righteous. If He were to give the unjust what they really deserved, they would be sentenced to a life absent from Him. But God seeks a relationship with the unjust as well as the just.

There was a time when you, one of the righteous, were one of the unrighteous. A time when Jesus Christ was not your sacrificial Lamb. A time when you were not walking with God. A time when you were living for yourself, not for God. What if God had given you what you deserved before you became just in His eyes? Before you were covered by the blood of Jesus Christ?

But He did not. He sent you rain and flowers while He waited patiently for you to become one of His. For you to become one of the just. And now, because of God's love, you can say with certainty that you are righteous – one of the just.

And the storms?

How will the unjust ever know how to handle the storms of life unless they see how the just handle them? How will they ever know who they are to go to when they need help if they never see who the just go? How will they ever witness the righteous kneeling before the Lord asking for His help unless they are beside them in the same storm? How will the unjust ever know that they are walking down the wrong path of life or even that there is another path to life unless they see how the just walk? How will the unjust ever see how God cares for His own unless they witness it?

Most importantly, how will the unjust ever know about Jesus unless they see Him through the just? Unless they see how the just weather their life storms. Unless they are able to watch how the just keep their eyes on Jesus while treading stormy waves?

And the flowers?

The next time you see a flower, pluck it and smell it. And thank God for this wonderful gift. Thank God for His love. For His storms. For His gentle rains. For His Son, Jesus, who is your sacrificial Lamb. And for His patience as He waited for you to become one of the just.

Romans 8:28

> And we know that all things work together
> for good to those who love God, to those
> who are called according to His purpose.
> (Romans 8:28 NKJV)

We often think of the trials God allows in our lives as tests. We often say God is testing us—testing our hearts, strength, and faith—through the trials He allows us walk through. But in reality, these trials are not God testing us to see just how strong our faith is or how much we love for Him. No. I do believe that God already knows those things for He knows our hearts.

These trials are for us. They show us how strong our faith is and how much we truly love God. They can be and often are wake up calls for us. They will show us just where our hearts are. And who or what we are truly relying on. They also show us just how strong our strengths are and how weak our weaknesses are. And - they will show us if we are walking with God – or if we are not. Eek!

Our trials give us glimpses of God working in our lives. And shows us that He not only can, but He will. Trials can, and will, increase our trust in God.

They can be times of deep walks with our Lord. Times of increased prayer. Increased seeking. Increased sensitivity.

They can be times of unexplainable peace, you know, the peace that passes all understanding.

They may also be times of completely emptying ourselves before God. Times of complete and unadulterated honesty when we tell all to God. Share all with God. As we never have before. A time when we fully surrendered to God and to God alone.

Our trials make us turn to God for what we need—love, acceptance, mercy, guidance, answers. We turn to God for a listening ear, for strength, and for healing. During these trials, we see the almighty hand of God move in our lives. We get to experience His awesome power. For God promised to take care of His own, and our trials are times that prove that promise.

Trials can cause us to be more thankful for what we have. Thankful for families both blood and Christian. Thankful for those whom God uses to administer to us. Thankful for Jesus's being our pathway to God. Trials will teach us how to look for and to anticipate the blessings of God.

Yes, trials are hard. But they need to be hard. Unfortunately, most of us remember that hard times in far greater detail that we do the soft times. We tend to learn more intently when placed between the rock and the hard spot. Trials increase our wisdom about God and about the things of God. Trials teach us. For there is usually a lesson in our trials. Lessons that will stay with us for a very long time.

So, as strange as this may sound, do not waste your trials. Allow them to help you grow in your spiritual walk. Let them draw you closer to God. Let them show you just how God can and will work for you. How He will care for you. How He loves you. God will use anything and anyone He needs to when caring for His children, be it people, pastors, sermons, and even ravens. (Yes, God sends ravens. Just ask Elijah.) God loves you very much. You are His child. And He is willing to do what He can for you.

Allow yourself to learn from your trials. For once you've made it through your trial, God will, at some time in your life, place someone in your path who is going through the same trial. God will use you to care for and mentor this person just as He used others to care for and mentor you as you were going through your trial. Without your trial, you would not have learned the lesson you are now passing on to another.

God is so wonderful. And trials are too.

Sin's Ripple

Throw a pebble into the middle of a lake and watch what happens. As the stone hits the water is causes ripples which are tight and high at the point of contact. Then the tight waves created by the pebble are followed by ripples which will travel quite some distance.

This ripple effect can also happen in our Christian family. We are told that as Christians, we are one body. That what affects one affects all. This affect can be from something as great as a wedding or a newborn or from something painful such as the loss of a loved one.

> For as we have many members in one body, but all the members do not have the same function, so we, being many, are one body in Christ, and individually members of one another. (Romans 12:4–5 NKJV)

But this affect does happen and does not stop with just one or two people. Just as the pebble causes ripples which move out from the point of contact, the affect moves out toward larger circles touching many lives on its way out.

And so, it is with sin. Sin affects the Christian body. From the pulpit down to the worker bees and the other way around. Sin can affect the entire Christian church. When one part, one member, or one person sins, the entire body feels the effect of that sin. Form the point of contact that sin ripples out touching everyone who is in the water. And sometimes, this rippling sin can cause great pain, sorrow, and even separation.

Let us look at Joshua 7. Because Achan had sinned against God, the entire nation of Israel tasted defeat in battle. When Achan and his family sinned against God, they tried to hide it, and in doing so, they lied. See the ripples of sin? Once you begin to live with unrepented sin, you need to hide it, causing you to lie. Which is yet another sin.

God was displeased with Achan's sin, and once Joshua found out about it, he was displeased as well. Joshua had Achan, his family, livestock, and his tent stoned, burned, and buried under rocks. The ripples of Achan's sin affected not only his family but also his cows, donkeys, sheep, and even his tent.

Everyone knows how David lusted after, pursued, and slept with another man's wife. How David's sin was done in darkness. Then when she was found to be with child, David's child, David tried to coerce her husband into having sexual relations with Bathsheba so others would think the child was the seed of Bathsheba's husband. Sin ripple!

However, David's best-laid plans did not happen. So, to hide his sin, David arranged the death of her husband who is an innocent man. Sin ripple! Adultery and manipulation. Lies and murder. Ripples, ripples, and more ripples of sin!

There is still one more sin ripple to this story. Bathsheba gave birth to David's son, but the Lord was displeased with David's sins and did not allow the son to live. David lost his firstborn son that Bathsheba bore to him. Big sin ripple! Ouch! (2 Samuel 11–12).

Sometimes, you may think that you can do this sin just this one time. No one will know. Just this once. It will not hurt anyone. But it does. It hurts a lot of people. You for one. And many others as well. You cannot have sin in your life without it affecting you and your relationship with God. Without it affecting your relationship with your family be it your blood family or your Christian family. And you can be sure your sin will be found out. God's Word tells us that whatever is done in darkness will be brought out to light for all to see.

> Therefore judge nothing before the time, until the Lord comes, who will both bring to light the hidden things of darkness and reveal the counsels of the hearts. Then each one's praise will come from God. (1 Corinthians 4:5 NKJV)

But even worse than that (if there can be a worse) is the effect our sin has on our Christian walk. How can you witness to someone that you have just lied to? Or have just cheated? Or maybe committed adultery with? How can you tell others that Jesus loves them when they have just witnessed your being harsh to others? Or why should others listen to you when you tell them they need Jesus Christ as their Savior if they've heard you gossiping?

Oh the ripples of sin!

Getting Ahead of God

Getting ahead of God and not waiting on God is dangerous territory. Every time I do something without waiting for God's assistance, I end up with a mess. God has warned us time and time again that we are to wait for Him. That we are much stronger, much wiser and could do so much more <u>when </u>we waited for Him. <u>But only</u> when we waited for Him.

We see this demonstrated in the lives of Abraham and Sarah as found in Genesis 15:1–9. God told Abraham that even in his old age, He would give him a son and that his descendants would be too many to count. God Himself said these things to Abraham!

I think perhaps Abraham may have told Sarah about that visit from God. I am sure that he was very excited about the visit from God and about the promise of a son who would be the first of many descendants. Too many to count descendants. What a promise! I would be excited, wouldn't you?

But then time went on and nothing happened. Month after month and still no child. Had God forgotten His promise to Abraham? It has been a while since God promised them a son.

It appears as if Sarah became tired of waiting for God. Maybe she was beginning to doubt God. Or maybe she was beginning to think that Abraham had made up the story of meeting with God and of God's promise. We are not told why, but Sarah took things into her own hands. She got ahead of God. She went to Abraham and told him to lay with her handmaiden, Hagar, so she could have a child by her. Yes, Sarah had gotten ahead of God and was asking Abraham to do the same.

Now before we put all the blame on Sarah, let us remember that Abraham was the one God had spoken the promised to. Scripture tells us that Abraham believed God. He believed that he would have a son and descendants whose numbers would match the number of the stars. And yet, when his wife told him to lie with Hagar, he did so willingly. He could have told his wife no. He could have told her that he believed God's promise and wanted to wait on Him. But he did not.

So, no one waited on God's promise. They acted in their own strength – their own judgement. And because of that, they created an issue that not only they had to deal with, but nations have had to deal with from that day forward. The union of Abraham and Hagar yielded the son named Ishmael, who was not the promised son.

Even before he was born, Ishmael was creating a great problem between Sarah, Abraham, and Hagar. There was great tension among the three. Sarah was being taunted by Hagar because Hagar was a mother and Sarah was not. Finally, Sarah went to Abraham and complained about Hagar. Complained about how bad Hagar was treating her. And even though it was her idea, Sarah blamed Abraham for the fact that Hagar was pregnant with his child. What this not the plan? That Hagar would bare a son to Abraham?

> So Sarai said to Abram, "See now, the LORD has restrained me from bearing children. Please, go in to my maid; perhaps I shall obtain children by her." And Abram heeded

the voice of Sarai. Then Sarai, Abram's wife, took Hagar her maid, the Egyptian, and gave her to her husband Abram to be his wife, after Abram had dwelt ten years on the land of Canaan.

So he went in to Hagar, and she conceived. And when she saw that she had conceived, her mistress became despised in her eyes. Then Sarai said to Abram, "My wrong be upon you! I gave my maid into your embrace; and when she saw that she had conceived, I became despised in her eyes. The LORD judge between you and me." (Genesis 16:2–4 NKJV)

Whoa! Had this not been Sarah's idea? Hadn't she asked Abraham to lie with Hagar? And now she was in his face complaining that Hagar was treating her badly? Really? And in order to bow out of this no-win situation, Abraham told Sarah to do as she wanted with Hagar. And Sarah does. She mistreats Hagar in such a vicious manner that Hagar ran away.

While Hagar was in the desert awaiting the death of her and her unborn, an angel came and told her that she was going to have a son and that she was to name him Ishmael. The angel told her that the son would be a wild man - a wild donkey of a man. The hand of Ishmael would be against every man and the hand of every man would be against Ishmael. And so, it is today. For it is commonly believed that Ishmael was the father of the Arabic nations.

Our - *Hurry up! Let's get 'er done!*- or - *Gotta help*

God - attitude affects not only us but others as well. And it can cause grief for many generations to come.

But our God is a merciful God. And patient. Even though Abraham and Sarah had messed up the first time, He is giving them a second chance. In Genesis 18, we see that He sent three men to tell Abraham (once again) that he would have a son and that his descendants would be far too many to count.

When Sarah overheard what the three men told Abraham, she laughed because she thought she was well past childbearing age (Genesis 18–9:14). Poor Sarah! Had she not learned her lesson? For what God says will happen - will happen. Period. But it will happen in God's timing. Not hers. Not Abraham's. Not yours. Not mine. But God's. And God's alone.

Before you come down on Sarah for her continued lack of faith that God would do as His promised, take a good look at yourself. Have you learned to wait on God? Or are there areas in your life in which you try to get ahead of God? Areas where you become impatient? Where you get tired of waiting for God? Areas where God seems to be dragging His feet? Where you just want to jump in and help Him?

Please, my fellow Christians, before you jump in to help, make sure that this is what God wants you to do. Before you set out to help anyone or anything, spend a few minutes, months, or even years in prayer, asking God for His desire in this situation. And then, listen to God.

Sometimes, we think we are helping when in fact we are just making a big mess. A fine example of this is when Sarah told Abraham to lie with Hagar so they could have heirs through a surrogate mother. From what I have read, this was a common practice in that day. But that was not what God wanted.

When you are tempted to try to help God, *stop. Drop to your knees. Pray for God's guidance. Listen for His voice. And wait on Him.* The consequences of getting ahead of God, of doing things on your timetable and not God's or of trying to do something relying on your strength and wisdom rather that God's can be dire. And they could last forever.

Do Atheists Really Exist?

Do atheist really exist? This question may seem silly. But if atheists believe there is not a God because they cannot see Him, then why do they call out to Him when they're in trouble? Why do they not call out to a tree, or a car, or to a human being they can see?

From what I have experienced, atheists believe that God does not exist because they cannot see Him. And since they cannot see Him, He cannot exist. When you try to reason with those who say they are atheists, they will use this type of reasoning.

However, let us apply this reasoning to the wind. Does it exist? Can you see? No. Wind cannot be seen. So, I ask if you cannot see wind, then how do you know it exist?

Wind cannot be seen, but we know it exist. For we can see the effects of wind, which means it exists. Just look at the results of high winds such as hurricanes or the straight winds of a thunderstorm. Even though we could not see the actual wind, we can see the very real effects of it. It is strange when atheists try to use nature to sustain their belief that God does not exist. For, by doing so, they are in essence, proving that God does actually exist. Because God's Word tells us it is through nature that we can see Him and know His ways.

> The heavens declare the glory of God; and the firmament shows His handiwork. (Psalm 19:1 NKJV)

It's true that we cannot see God as we see other human beings. But we can see the effects of God. We see God in the beauty of nature. In the orderly way God has orchestrated nature. We see God in the lives of others who are walking their Christian talk. We may even on occasion, see His hand in the way of a miracle. Those of us who have accepted Jesus as our Savior can see God's effect in very visible ways.

Atheists or those who call themselves such may not be able to see God's effect as Christians do. God's Word tells us that those who are not of God cannot see or understand the things of God. That those who are not of God will find the things of God foolish.

> But the natural man does not receive the things of the Spirit of God, for they are foolishness to him; nor can he know them, because they are spiritually discerned. (1 Corinthians 2:14 NKJV)

Atheists are telling you what their intellects are telling them. If you cannot see God, God must not exist. Period.

However, according to the above Scripture, if atheists cannot understand the things of God, they must not be of God. And since they are not of God, they must belong to Satan who has his fingers in their ears and his hands over their eyes. Satan wants to keep them from hearing God's voice or seeing God's ways because the moment God becomes real to them, Satan will no longer be their father. God will be.

However, we as Christians are to love those who claim to be atheists. Jesus told us to do so. This does not mean that we are to embrace their viewpoint. However, this does mean that we are to remember that they were created in the image of God just as we were. And Jesus died for their sins just as He died for ours.

By remembering these things with our actions, we are displaying the true life of a Christian. A Christian life that will give the atheist something to think about. Deep down in the soul of everyone is an instinctive knowledge of God. In this inner soul, God has placed a need to worship. A need for Him. Only when we fully surrender our lives to God through the blood of Jesus are these areas in our souls filled and satisfied.

So, I ask again.

Do - atheist really exist?

Or - are they merely souls who are lost?

You Are Not to Fear Man

We are <u>told</u> – no allow me to rephrase that - we are <u>warned</u> - by God to not fear man but to trust Him instead.

> The fear of man brings a snare, but whoever trusts in the LORD shall be safe. (Proverbs 29:25 NKJV)

> It is better to trust in the LORD than to put confidence in man. (Psalm 118:8 NKJV)

These are just a few of the many verses in the Bible regarding fear of man vs. trust in God. I have listed some more scriptures at the bottom of this article that confirm this warning.

The Bible tells us why God is so concerned with our fear of man. In Genesis 12, the Lord told Abram that he was to leave his homeland and go to another land. However, God did not name the land. Instead, God promised to make Abram a great nation and to bless his name. God told Abram that whoever blessed him God would bless.

> I will make you a great nation; I will bless you and make your name great; and you shall be a blessing. I will bless those who bless you, and I will curse him who curses you; and in you all the families of the earth shall be blessed. (Genesis 12:2–3 NKJV)

So, Abram left his homeland with his family including Lot, his nephew, and headed for Canaan. After arriving there, he traveled through the land going as far as the great tree of Moreh at Shechem, which was a land occupied by the Canaanites. The Lord came to Abram again with another promise.

> Then the LORD appeared to Abram and said, "To your descendants I will give this land." And there he built an altar to the LORD, who had appeared to him. (Genesis 12:7 NKJV)

Abram continued to travel toward the Negev and then onto Egypt because a famine had fallen on the land. As he and Sarai, his wife, were about to enter Egypt, Abram became fearful for his life. His wife was a woman of great beauty, and Abram feared that if the Egyptians knew she was his wife, they would kill him so that they could have her. So, he told Sarai to tell the Egyptians that she was his sister.

When Abram and Sarai arrived in Egypt, the Egyptians saw how beautiful she was. Some of Pharaoh's officials told him of her great beauty, so Pharaoh took her into his palace to be his wife. He gave Abram sheep and cattle for Sarai. And why not? For all Pharaoh knew, Abram and Sarai were brother and sister. But the Lord knew the truth. The Lord knew that Abram and Sarai had lied about their relationship. That in fact they were husband and wife, not brother and sisters. And even though the Pharaoh did not know, God still inflicted serious diseases on Pharaoh and his house because of Sarai.

Scripture does not tell how Pharaoh found out about

Abram and Sarai – that they were truly husband and wife and not sister and brother. But he did. Pharaoh then summoned Abram and asked him why he had lied about Sarai being his sister and why he had allowed Pharaoh to take her as his wife. Abram was facing an angry Pharaoh. Because of his fear of the Egyptians, because of his fear of man, he had lied, had asked his wife to lie and is now finding himself in danger of losing his life.

The angry Pharaoh kicked Abram and all his possessions out of Egypt. And rightfully so. Innocent people had suffered because of Abram's fear of man. Pharaoh had been lied to. He had taken another man's wife to be his wife. He and his family are stricken with serious diseases. All because Abram had feared man.

Poor Abram. If only he had trusted God. He did when God asked him to travel to an unknown land. If only he had trusted God one more time for his protection from the Egyptians, rather than cowering in fear of man. Where did all his fearlessness and faith in God go when he entered into Egypt? Did Abram not believe God's promise that those who would curse would be cursed by God? And that this curse included the Egyptians? I will bless those who bless you, and I will curse those who curse you; and in you all the families of the earth shall be blessed.

You and I are often like Abram. We forget what God has done for us. We forget about the times God has protected and has comforted us. We forget the promises He has made to us. And sometimes, sadly, we can at times even forget who our sacrificial Lamb is. That because of Jesus's blood we are now God's children. Sometimes our remembering just does not work very well, and we follow in the footstep of Abram. Not good. For not placing our trust in God's promises, will create messes. Big messes. And can affect others in a very negative way. Every time.

Ouch!

We must remember to not fear man <u>but</u> to trust God. And to trust in God's promises. We must remember that when God makes a promise - He keeps it. For God cannot lie.

> The LORD is on my side; I will not fear. What can man do to me? (Psalm 118:6 NKJV)

> "Listen to Me, you who know righteousness, you people in whose heart is My law; do not fear the reproach of men, nor be afraid of their insults. For the moth will eat them up like a garment, and the worm will eat them like wool; but My righteousness will be forever, and My salvation from generation to generation." (Isaiah 51:7–8 NKJV)

> Let your conduct be without covetousness; be content with such things as you have. For He Himself has said, "I will never leave you nor forsake you." So we may boldly say: "The LORD is my helper; I will not fear. What can man do to me?" (Hebrews 13:5–6 NKJV)

Just Rest?

Jesus has always been our leader in all things. Not only in spiritual things, but in money things, and in relationship things, In all of life's things. While walking the earth Jesus was quite busy. For He had many things to teach, many healings to do and many people to attend to. However, Scripture tells us of times when Jesus would go off to be by His self. To take time away from the crowds, from the day's business and from the demands of His followers. Time to pray and to rest.

> So He Himself often withdrew into the wilderness and prayed. (Luke 5:16 NKJV)

If Jesus, who was the Son of God, escaped the hustle and bustle of His busy days to pray and rest, why do we not do the same? We, as Christians, are to follow in Jesus's footsteps. And if Jesus took time to rest then so should we. In Genesis we find that God rested on the seventh day after creating the heavens and earth.

> And on the seventh day God ended His work which He had done, and He rested on the seventh day from all His work which He had done. (Genesis 2:2 NKJV)

Our Heavenly Father, the Almighty God, rested once His work was done. But for some reason we, the created, seem to think we are not to take time off from the demands of our jobs and life to rest, to pray, and worship. But if God and Jesus took time to rest, then should we not do the same?

God wants us to take time to rest. He commanded us to rest.

> "Six days you shall work, but on the seventh day you shall rest; in plowing time and in harvest you shall rest." (Exodus 34:21 NKJV)

God commanded that even our animals were to rest.

> "Six days you shall do your work, and on the seventh day you shall rest, that your ox and your donkey may rest, and the son of your female servant and the stranger may be refreshed." (Exodus 23:12 NKJV)

Rest renews us mentally and physically. Rest gives us a new spin on our cares. Rest is a time for slowing down, for reflection, and for worship. And it just plain ol' feels good to rest. To have a "veggy" day as I call it.

But true rest is more than sitting in front of the TV. Or lack of physical movement. True rest requires that we are one hundred percent trusting that God is there with us watching over us and keeping us from harm. Resting is truly trusting that God will never leave us and take care of us. Always.

Resting in the Lord also means not trying to do everything in your strength. It means that you stop trying to control everything. You stop trying to do your part *and* God's part. You allow God to be in control

Resting, true resting, means you accept the peace Jesus offers you. That peace that exceeds all understanding.

So, when you come across thing that do not make sense, and you will, you can rest assured that God is working all things for your good. And this rest comes from the peace that Jesus offers.

Please allow me to ask a few probing questions. What is keeping you from truly resting? From entering your hiding place promised to you by God. Is it pride? That old' "I can do it myself"? Or the suborn attitude of "Without me, the world would fall apart"? Are you afraid that you if retreat from the world and its demands, even for a few hours, you may lose control over things in your life?

I struggle with this control issue. And I must frequently remind myself that God is the only one who truly has control over anything. I only *think* I do. The only thing I really have any control over is my choice of how I will respond to the present moment. And to whom I will worship, honor and serve. Over other things I have very little control. If any.

So, please my fellow Christian, follow the example of our Savior. Make time every day to rest. If the day has been a very hard day, crawl up into Jesus's lap and rest in His love. Rest in His peace. That's what I do.

My Scripture Blanket Made from Scraps

I love to crochet. It's a great way to relax. I give away most of the items I make. Some I have sold. However, I have kept one item for myself. My scripture blanket made from scraps.

To make it, I made as many squares as I wanted using yarn scraps from other projects, and that created some really great color combinations. Make your squares any size and any color using your favorite stitch. Remember, this is your creation.

Sew the squares together in a way that best suits your taste, embroider them with your favorite scriptures, then your favorite style of border for a finished look. For this is truly your creation.

When you find more Scripture that you would like to include in your blanket, make more squares, sew them on, and embroider them. Once your blanket is just the right size you will have all your favorite Bible verses in one place. And on a blanket that you can wrap around your shoulders. *Ahhh!* Yes. You are now covered in Scripture. Doesn't that feel good?

When I'm fearful or in a hard spot, I wrap up in my scripture blanket. I envelop myself in God's Word. In God's love. I know that God loves me without this blanket, but the blanket is a very touchable reminder of just how much God does love me.

My scripture blanket not only offers me physical comfort but emotional comfort as well. The scriptures on it are God's promises to me. Promises to never leave me. To never to forsake me. To always have great plans for me. To work all things for my good. Promises to love me and take care of me. Promises from God that I am special to Him.

And God does not lie. I can take Him at His Word and trust what He says. I can rely on what God tells me. And you can too.

Just as I make scripture blanket squares from what would be otherwise thrown away, God does the same thing. He takes those who seem to be life's throw aways and do something great through them. He takes the scraps of life and makes something beautiful out of them.

We have all at some time or another felt like throwaways. We have all felt the knife-wielding pain of rejection. The burning pain of stabbing words. The heartache of belittlement. We all are now or have lived in hard times. Times when we were torn apart emotionally and maybe even physically.

But take heart, my fellow Christians. God, who sees these things, can and will take care of you. He will lift you up. He will heal you. He loves you that much. He will take the scraps of your hard times and weave a unique and beautiful creation. A one-of-a-kind creation made by Him just for Him. A creation that pleases Him. And who knows more about creating than the Creator of everything?

Just look at the beauty He created out of the throwaways in the Bible.

1. The woman at the well who was living in an immoral manner for she had had husbands and was now just living with a man. And yet after her encounter

with Jesus, she became an evangelist and won many souls for Him in her hometown.

2. Saul made it his personal mission to find and kill as many Christians as he could. Scriptures tell us that he hunted them down and was on his way to do so again, when he was converted and became Paul. The man who wrote most of the New Testament.

3. Simon Peter, one of Jesus's disciples. Probably one of my favorite disciples. He is still known as the disciple who denied knowing Jesus three times. And yet, in the Book of Acts we are told how he was filled with the Holy Spirit and brought thousands of souls to salvation with just one sermon.

All these people were once fragments, scraps, throwaways if you will. And yet God created something very wonderful from these fragments, scraps, throwaways. God can and will do the same in your life. He is not a respecter of persons; He does not love any one of us more than others.

Fellow Christians, God can take the ratty pieces of your life—the scraps of a painful relationship - the throwaway feelings of being unloved and rejected—and make something unique, beautiful, and useful out of them. God has promised us all that He will work out all things for our best. Maybe not what we have asked for, but what we need. What is best for us.

> And we know that all things work together for good to those who love God, to those who are the called according to His purpose. (Romans 8:28 NKJV)

God has promised not to harm us. But to give us a hope and a future. And to hear and answer our heart-sent prayers.

> For I know the thoughts I think toward you, says the LORD, thoughts of peace and not of evil, to give you a future and a hope. Then you will call upon Me and go and pray to Me, and I will listen to you. And you will seek Me and find Me, when you search for Me with all your heart. (Jeremiah 29:11–13 NKJV)

God has promised to sustain you.

> Cast your burden on the LORD, and He shall sustain you; He shall never permit the righteous to be moved. (Psalm 55:22 NKJV)

God is not only the Almighty God who spoke the earth and its inhabitants into being, but He is a just God. And as a just God He cannot lie. So what God says – whatever He promises - He will do.

Gifts

You have been shopping for that perfect Christmas gift for a very special person. You want something that shows just how much you love them. So, you look and look and look until you find it—that perfect gift. You present that perfect gift to your very special person and eagerly await, watching for their expression of surprise and delight. What a magical moment that makes all that shopping worth it!

Remember how you could hardly wait for Christmas to arrive when you were a child? And then there it was! A morning when the living room was filled to its capacity with gifts wrapped in Christmas paper. Or perhaps it was that magical Christmas morning when your most treasured desire was leaning against the wall next to the Christmas tree looking all new and shiny.

Remember how the Christmas tree was lit up? How Christmas decorations were everywhere? How the room was filled with laughter? Remember your excitement as you sifted through the mountains of gifts looking for yours and being joyful when you found them?

You eagerly tore off the wrapping paper. Your excitement was electric! As you ripped open present after present, you said, "Thank you, Mom and Dad! Thank you, Aunt Shirley and Uncle Cliff! Thank you, sister! Thank you, brother!" And maybe even a "Thank you, Jesus!" How happy you were!

Moms and dads, remember how happy it made you feel to see your little ones so excited, so squealy, and so alive? Remember how their untethered joy and excitement made all the shopping and late-night gift-wrapping worth it. Remember how the two hours of sleep somehow did not matter?

But what if that very special person you bought that special gift for unwraps it, and just puts it aside? What if they appear to not like it? What if they do not even mumble a simple thank you? Or they tell you that it's not what they had wanted? All the hours of shopping now appear as though they were wasted. All that effort for not. How disappointing.

Or even worse yet, as if that were possible, they do not even unwrap your perfect gift? What if they ignore your gift and all the effort you put into finding it and presenting it? Would you feel rejected? Unwanted? Unloved? Unimportant?

Most of us are far more gracious than that when it comes to receiving gifts from others. Most of us would at the very least say thank you to the giver. But what about God's gifts? What are you doing with His gifts? With the gifts He has given you?

In 1 Corinthians 12:1–11, we read that God gives us gifts. And He gives us the gifts that He wants us to have. Right away we think of His Son, our Savior, Jesus Christ. But God gives us so much more. He gives us gifts that enable us to do what He asks us to do. He gives us gifts to bring us joy. Gifts that satisfy our hearts' desires. Gifts that fulfill our innermost beings. Wonderful gifts. Perfect gifts. Eternal gifts. His gifts.

And everyone's gift is different. They may be in the same category as others such as the gift for music, teaching, or leadership. But even within the same realm everyone's gifts are different. They have been customized by God for that individual. No two gifts are the same because God's children are not the same.

May I ask again - what are you doing with the gifts God has given to you? Do you eagerly search for them as you searched for Christmas gifts? Do find them exciting? Exhilarating? Soothing? Like they were made just for you? Do you eagerly accept them?

When God give you a gift, please treasure it. Although you may think you want the same gift that God has given to another, please try your gift on for size. You will find that your gift fits more much better than someone's gift.

And please try not to do what I have done, placed God's gifts on a shelf. And even worse, I placed on the shelf unopened. This gift was from God, my Creator. My heavenly Father. And yet I did not even lift the lid to see what was inside. How sad this must have made my Heavenly Father. He wants to shower us with gifts because He loves us. Perfect gifts for His special people.

All of God's gifts are just as big and as exciting as the gifts that were under the Christmas tree. And guess what, there is no waiting for Christmas here, folks. God gives us gifts all year long because He loves us and wants us to be happy. He wants us to have the gifts we need to do the things that He asks us to do.

God knows what our perfect gifts are. He knows our sizes, our favorite colors, and just how to wrap them. He knows our innermost being and our desires. He knows our wants and our needs – and our hearts.

I believe God finds great pleasure when we use the gifts that He has given us. I believe that God finds it very pleasant watching His children using their gifts. I also believe that it greatly touches God's heart when He hears one of His children say, "Thank you, Father, for your gift. I love it. It's perfect." While Scripture does not tell us that our Heavenly Father physically smiles, I can just imagine one on His face as I sit here writing this very article. Or when I play music for His children. For these are the gifts He has given to me.

God's tailor-made gifts enable us to do the work He has asked us to do. His gifts satisfy that deep-down burning desire inside us. God's gifts bring us joy and peace and a sense of well-being. God's gifts last for an eternity. And God's gifts are good. Very good.

The Desert

It's easy to be critical of those who had to wander in the desert for forty years. I wonder how the Israelites could have been so doubtful of God's mercy and ability to care for them. Did He not instruct them to put lambs' blood on their doorways marking their homes as that of Israelites and not Egyptians so the angel of death would pass over them? Did God not free them from the slavery imposed on them by Pharaoh and the Egyptians? Did He not part the Red Sea for them and then drown the pursuing Egyptians?

And yet when they were faced with another challenge, the Israelites began to moan and groan. Makes you just want to ask, "Really? I mean, come on, folks! What's wrong with you? Have you not just witnessed a bunch of miracles?"

But before you come down too hard on the Israelites, take a long look at your life. When you're wandering your desert, what do you do? Do you moan and groan because it is too hard? Or too hot? Do you complain about eating that same ol' manna again? Do you whine, "If only things could be different. If only they could be like they used to be"?

I do. When God saves my household from the angel of death, I am one of the first to stand up and say "Yeah! God is good!" And when God parts the Red Sea for me, I run across the dry land with my hands up yelling, "God is so good! And as I watch God destroying my enemy, I bask in the knowledge that He has my back.

But when I go back into my desert and start facing trials and challenges again …When I have to eat that same ol' manna day after day again … I tend to forget what God has done for me. So, instead of yelling, "God is so good!" I struggle to come up with a whispered and flat "Oh, wow." I no longer sing praises to my Lord. I don't feel like it. My enthusiasm is all gone.

Who wants to yell praises to God when they're enduring extreme desert heat? When was the last time you heard someone say, "Wow! God is so good to me! He has me in the desert again! *Yahoo!* I love it! All this heat and thirst and heavy toil. Yea bring it on!"

But the only way you can survive in the desert is by praising God. Nothing else will work. You need to throw your hands up and sing His praises. Only by worshipping God and God alone will you be able to withstand the intense heat. To survive your desert graciously, you must tell God how much you love Him in spite of your pain and suffering. You must continue to praise God with your heart, soul, mind, and voice. God likes to hear your praises, but you also need to hear yourself singing praise songs.

If your pain and suffering get bigger and last longer, your praises to God should get bigger and last longer. You need to acquire a taste for manna and be sure to thank God for it. Remember that God has allowed you to walk on dry land through a sea to free you. Remember how He watched your back and destroyed those who wanted to destroy you. Remember that you have something the Israelites did not to help you through the desert—your Bible and the Holy Spirit.

The Israelites could not read Exodus 17 and learn that Moses would strike a rock and water would come forth. They had to live the events as they unfolded without any prior knowledge that God was going to help them.

I am so thankful that the Lord gave me His Word

in written form. Although I may not be able to foresee how future events will play out, I do know from reading about past events that God will care for His own. And I do know that the very moment I accepted Jesus I became one of His.

Jesus Completes the Law

Hear, O Israel: The LORD our God, the LORD is one. Love the LORD your God with all your heart and with all your soul and with all your strength. These commandments that I give you today are to be upon your hearts. Impress them on your children. Talk about them when you sit at home and when you walk along the road, when you lie down and when you get up. Tie them as symbols on your hands and bind them on your foreheads. Write them on the doorframes of your houses and on your gates. (Deuteronomy 6:4–9 NIV)

"The LORD commanded us to obey all these decrees and to fear the LORD our God, so that we might always prosper and be kept alive, as is the case today. And if we are careful to obey all this law before the LORD our God, as he commanded us, that will be our righteousness." (Deuteronomy 6:24–25 NIV)

This scripture follows the Ten Commandments. Moses was telling the Israelites to love only the Lord their God. Moses warned the nation not to stray from the laws of God. Obeying God will give them long and prosperous lives. And obeying God's laws would be their righteousness.

Now look at this.

> Hearing that Jesus had silenced the Sadducees, the Pharisees got together. One of them, an expert in the law, tested him with this question: "Teacher, which is the greatest commandment in the Law?"
>
> Jesus replied: "'Love the Lord your God with all your heart and with all your soul and with all your mind.' This is the first and greatest commandment. And the second is like it: 'Love your neighbor as yourself.' All the Law and the Prophets hand on these two commandments." (Matthew 22:34–40 NIV)

Did you see that? Jesus was reciting scripture from Deuteronomy! To which you say, "Ah, yes. Of course, He did! Jesus was a Jew. And Jews were raised on Old Testament scripture." So?

Well, this will blow your socks off. There was so much more to Jesus than just another Jew who could recite Old Testament Scripture. And He was so much more than a well-known healer or a great teacher.

> Jesus went throughout Galilee, teaching in their synagogues, preaching the good news of the kingdom, and healing every disease and sickness among the people. (Matthew 4:23 NIV)

And this is what Jesus had to say:

"Do not think that I have come to abolish the Law or the Prophets; I have not come to abolish them but to fulfill them. I tell you the truth, until heaven and earth disappear, not the smallest letter, not the least stroke of a pen, will be any means disappear from the Law until everything is accomplished. Anyone who breaks one of the least of these commandments and teaches others to do the same will be called least in the kingdom of heaven, but whoever practices and teaches these commands will be called great in the kingdom of heaven. For I tell you that unless your righteousness surpasses that of the Pharisees and the teachers of the law, you will certainly not enter the kingdom of heaven." (Matthew 5:17–20 NIV)

Yes. Jesus, our righteousness, was here to fulfill the Old Testament law, not to replace it. And if you look very carefully, you will see again the same law and the same warning given to God's people during Moses' day.

The law: Love the Lord your God with all your heart, mind, and soul—with all your being. Love others as you love yourself. Love your neighbors as if they were you.

The warning: If we fail to do so, we will not have eternal life in heaven.

Unless we follow the law that God has given us, unless we obey the law Jesus came to fulfill, we cannot be seen by God as being righteous. If we love the Lord our God with all our heart, mind and soul; and we love others as much as we love ourselves, then we will be viewed as being righteous in the eyes of God. And that is something I desire – greatly desire. Righteousness.

> For the LORD watches over the way of the righteous, but the way of the wicked will perish. (Psalm 1:6 NIV)

God told Moses that our obedience to His law equaled our righteousness in His eyes. Then Jesus told us that He came to fulfill the law. And He did so by becoming our blood sacrifice for our sins. So, only when God looks at us through His Son's blood do, we appear righteous in the sight of God. Only through our faith in who Jesus is do we become righteous.

For the blood of our Savior, Jesus, has washed away our sin and with it our unrighteousness. Because Jesus died as our Sin Lamb, the Almighty, the God who is just, can now look down upon us. Because of Jesus's obedience unto death, we can have a relationship with our Heavenly Father.

Thank you Jesus.

> But now a righteousness from God, apart from law, has been made known, to which the Law and the Prophets testify. This righteousness from God comes through faith in Jesus Christ to all who believe. There is no difference, for all have sinned and fall short of the glory of God, and are justified freely by his grace through the redemption that came by Christ Jesus. (Romans 3:21–24 NIV)

Scriptures Confirmed

Luke 4:1–13 tells us that Jesus was tempted by Satan in the desert.

> Then Jesus, being filled with the Holy Spirit, returned from the Jordan and was led by the Spirit into the wilderness, being temped for forty days by the devil. And in those days He ate nothing, and afterward, when they had ended, He was hungry.

> And the devil said to Him, "If You are the Son of God, command this stone to become bread." But Jesus answered him, saying, "It is written, 'Man shall not live by bread alone, but by every word of God.'"

> Then the devil, taking Him up on a high mountain, showed Him all the kingdoms of the world in a moment of time. And the devil said to Him, "All this authority I will give You, and their glory; for this has been delivered for me, and I give it to whomever I wish. Therefore, if You will worship before me, all will be Yours,"

> And Jesus answered and said, "Get behind Me, Satan! For is it written, 'You shall worship the LORD your God, and Him only you will serve.'"

Then he brought Him to Jerusalem, set Him on the pinnacle of the temple, and said to Him, "If You are the Son of God, throw Yourself down from here. For it is written: 'He shall give His angels charge over you, to keep you, and, in their hands they shall bear you up, lest you dash your foot against a stone.'"

And Jesus answered and said to him, "It has been said, 'You shall not tempt the LORD your God.'"

Now when the devil had ended every temptation, he departed from Him until an opportune time. (Luke 4:1–13 NKJV)

When pastors preach on this passage, we often hear about how Jesus battled with Satan and won. But I see so much more in this passage. I see scriptures being confirmed.

We are told that Jesus had been with God from the beginning.

In the beginning was the Word, and the Word was with God, and the Word was God. He was in the beginning with God. (John 1:1–2 NKJV)

And that Jesus was the Word that was with God.

And the Word became flesh and dwelt among us, and we beheld His glory, the glory as of the only begotten of the Father, full of grace and truth. (John 1:14 NKJV)

In God's Word Jesus Himself tells us that Satan was cast from heaven.

Then the seventy returned with joy, saying, "Lord, even the demons are subject to us in Your name." And He said to them, "I saw Satan fall like lightning from heaven." (Luke 10:17-18 NKJV)

Since Satan was in heaven at one time, and Jesus has been there from the beginning of time, it only makes sense that Satan knew who Jesus was. He knew that Jesus was God's Son.

He also knew that Jesus sits at the right hand of the Almighty God. Nonetheless, he went after Jesus in the desert. We read that he tempted – or rather tried to tempt Jesus – three times in the desert. How arrogant of Satan. Going after the Son of God!

However, let us heed this as a warning. If Satan is bold enough to go after Jesus, he has no problem coming after us. Compared to Jesus we are small game. An easy catch. Easy prey. God warned us about Satan. About his ways. God tells us that Satan is deceptive and is seeking someone to devour. Not just knock down – but to devour.

Be sober, be vigilant; because your adversary the devil walks around like a roaring lion, seeking whom he may devour. (1 Peter 5:8 NKJV)

God's Word also show us how to combat the wiles of Satan. Jesus was filled with the Holy Spirit before He went into the desert. Before He encountered Satan's wiles.

This shows us that being filled with the Holy Spirit gives us the ability to resist Satan's schemes. To know Satan's schemes. Like the thoughts he tries to put in our minds. And the way he sits on our shoulders whispering lies in our ears.

God's Word shows us that Jesus used scripture to combat Satan's suggestions. Please take note that Satan's comments were also from scripture. For Satan knows scripture maybe better than you and I. But he abuses it. He misquotes it. Satan will twist God's Word so it will appear as though he is right. To make you think God really did mean what he – Satan - says it means. He will not only misquote, but he will take it out of content or leave some words out. Or will use it incorrectly. Therefore, it is extremely important to know scripture. And to know it intimately. It must be imprinted in our minds and implanted in our hearts. And in our souls.

> Your word I have hidden in my heart, that
> I may not sin against You. (Psalm 119:11
> NKJV)

In order to know when God's Word is being abused, we need to stay in the Word daily if not hourly. And we need to keep our prayer life alive. To this day Satan still uses the scriptures abusively. He still misquotes. And he uses this to enter our churches. We are warned over and over to be on our guard. And we are also instructed on how to know false teachers.

Satan masquerades as an angel of light. It is not surprising then to find his servants in our churches masquerading as angels of light. As servants of righteousness. And God's Word has promised us many times that their end will be what their actions have determined they deserve. In other words, they will reap what they sow.

> For such are false apostles, deceitful workers, transforming themselves into apostles of Christ. And no wonder! For Satan himself transforms himself into an angel of light. Therefore it is no great thing if his ministers also transform themselves into ministers of righteousness, whose end will be according to their works. (2 Corinthians 11:13–15 NKJV)

In Luke, we read that Jesus stood firm against Satan and was the only one left standing after Satan fled. Thus, not only demonstrating how true this is, but confirming this will truly happen.

> Therefore submit to God. Resist the devil and he will flee from you. (James 4:7 NKJV)

But the sweetest and perhaps most important part of this scripture is the confirmation of not only *who* Jesus is, but also *what* Jesus is. Confirmation that Jesus is our sacrificial Lamb - pure, holy, without spot or blemish. In other words - without sin. Confirmation that when Jesus willingly bled for us on the cross, He was being our perfect, sinless, sacrificial Lamb that God required for the remission of our sins. Jesus's encounter with Satan in the desert proved that He did indeed meet the requirement

set forth for the sacrificial lamb – a male who was perfect –
who was without blemish.

As odd as this sounds, if Satan had not tempted Jesus in
the desert, then we would not only know for sure that Jesus
was indeed our blood sacrifice, but we would not know for
sure that Jesus did indeed know what temptation felt like.
That Jesus is indeed our High Priest who can sympathize
with our weaknesses.

> For we do not have a High Priest who cannot
> sympathize with our weaknesses, but was in
> all points tempted as we are, yet without sin.
> (Hebrews 4:15 NKJV)

This confrontation between Jesus and Satan should
teach us that Satan will try to deceive anyone and that
he comes to devour us when we are at our weakest. When
we are vulnerable. Or alone. Through this confrontation,
Jesus showed us that we are to prepare ourselves for these
confrontations by staying attuned to the Holy Spirit. And
Jesus showed us that once we have prepared ourselves by
being filled with the Holy Spirit, we are to just stand on
the Word of God. The true Word of God.

This is what Jesus did. When Jesus had resisted all
of Satan's temptations, Satan left the scene. Then God's
angels came and administered to Jesus. And the same
should happen for us. When we stand firm on God's Word
using it correctly, and Satan sees that he is not getting
anywhere with us, he may leave. At least for a little while.
And then, our Heavenly Father will send us comfort. Maybe
not angels as He did for Jesus, but He *will* comfort us.

Satan's actions in the desert confirm that God's Word
is real. That our Bible is the Word of God. In a strange

way, Satan's confrontation with Jesus in the desert helps us understand scripture. Helps us to know in our hearts that every Word in the Bible is the true Word *of* God. The true Word *from* God. Written *for* us. Given to us. A love letter from our Heavenly Father that will help us, guard us, and guide us in this life on earth.

What a wonderful God we serve.

If

Luke 4:1–13 show us how Satan operates. As one of my favorite pastors taught, Satan did not tell Jesus to "prove" that He was the Son of God or "since" He was the Son of God but "if" He was the Son of God ...

If. Such a small word with such a huge impact. How many times have you used it today? If I had only done ... If I had only said ... If I had gone .... If I had ... But what Satan was really saying to Jesus is if He was God's Son, this would happen. And if He was truly the Son of God then this would happen. Then, filled with arrogance, Satan took Jesus to a mountain top. He then told Jesus that should He bow down and worship him, he would give Jesus all the land that could be seen from that mountain top. Like really? Satan was going to give Jesus, the One who was there at the beginning. Remember what John 1:1 tells us?

And Satan is still saying the same thing today, isn't he? If you are really one of God's children, this will happen. If you are one of God's children, this would not have happened. Don't let Satan whisper that two-letter word in your ear...*if. If* God loves you ... *If* you were truly saved ... *If* you do this only this one time. You know the ifs. You've heard them. I have too.

Let's look at the ifs Satan whispers in our ears. Remember that Satan is not just a liar; he is the father of liars.

If God really loves you.

God knew you would wander from Him, would place things before Him, and even turn from Him for a while as you walk life's path, but He still loves you enough to give you His Son as your sacrificial sin Lamb to remit your sins. God did not just tell us He loved us. He showed He loved us. In the word of our Savior, Jesus,

> For God so loved the world that He gave His only begotten Son, that whoever believes in Him should not perish but have everlasting life. For God did not send His Son into the world to condemn the world, but that the world through Him may be saved. (John 3:16–17 NKJV)

If you are truly saved.

If we believe Jesus is our sacrificial sin Lamb who died on a cross to atone for our sins, we are saved and we bear the mark of God. God's Word tells us that the second we accept Jesus Christ as our Savior, we are marked with His seal.

> Now He who establishes us with you in Christ and has anointed us is God, who also has sealed us and given us the Spirit in our hearts as a guarantee. (2 Corinthians 21–22 NKJV)

> In Him you also trusted, after you heard the word of truth, the gospel of your salvation; in whom also, having believed, you were sealed with the Holy spirit of promise, who is the guarantee of our inheritance until the redemption of the purchased possession, to the praise of His glory. (Ephesians 1:13–14 NKJV)

And then there is one of Satan's greatest lies.

Do you really think you are good enough for God? Good enough to do God's work?

God's Word tells us that if He gives us a job to do, He will equip us for it. If He wants us to do something that costs money, He will finance it. God will not give us missions for which He has not given what we need including the strength to accomplish it.

You may find the task lying before you daunting and intimidating. But I promise you, if you ask the Lord for help and place your foot on the pathway that lies before you, God will be there for you. Guaranteed. How can I be so sure? The fact that you are reading these words is a testimony of what God can do. You see, I believe I am fulfilling a mission God has asked me to do. Every time I sit with my laptop, I ask the Lord to help me do what He has asked of me. And He does.

> ... being confident of this very thing, that He who has begun a good work in you will complete it unto the day of Jesus Christ. (1 Philippians 1:6 NKJV)

Strong Drink

Alcoholic beverages can be a sticky subject among saints. Some believe that drinking to excess is a sin, and others believe that drinking *any* alcohol is a sin. Let us see what God says about drinking alcohol.

> Give strong drink to him who is perishing, and wine to those who are bitter of heart. Let him drink and forget his poverty, and remember his misery no more. (Proverbs 31:6–7 NKJV)

> No longer drink only water, but use a little wine for your stomach's sake and your frequent infirmities. (1 Timothy 5:23 NKJV)

> It is not for kings, O Lemuel. It is not for kings to drink wine, nor for princes intoxicating drink; lest they drink and forge the law, and pervert the justice of all the afflicted. (Proverbs 31:4–6 NKJV)

We are warned that too much strong drink is not good for us because it will cause us sorrows, woes, and unnecessary wounds. Too much strong drink bites like a snake and causes us to see things that are not there and to do things that we would not ordinarily do.

Who has woes? Who has sorrow? Who has contentions? Who has complaints? Who has wounds without cause? Who has redness of eyes?

Who has woe? Who has sorrow? Who has
contentions? Who has complaints? Who has
wounds without cause? Who has redness of
eyes?

Those who linger long at the wine, those
who go in search of mixed wine. Do not look
on the wine when it is red, when it sparkles
in the cup, when it swirls around smoothly;
at the last it bites like a serpent, and stings
like a viper. Your eyes will see strange things,
and your heart will utter perverse things.
(Proverbs 23:29–33 NKJV)

But the following scripture goes much further. It warns
us of what our rewards are if we allow the consumption
of strong drink to become a way of life. If we allow it to
become something we must have to deal with life. If it
becomes a crutch. Or an idol. If it replaces God.

Now the works of the flesh are evident, which
are: adultery, fornication, uncleanness,
lewdness, idolatry, sorcery, hatred,
contentions, jealousies, outbursts of wrath,
selfish ambitions, dissensions, heresies,
envy, murders, drunkenness, revelries, and
the like; of which I tell you beforehand, just
as I also told you in time past, that those
who practice such things will not inherit the
kingdom of God. (Galatians 5:19–21 NKJV)

Did you see that? This scripture puts drunkenness
right next to murder and in the same list as sorcery. We

all know that murder is wrong and that playing around with sorcery is playing with fire. But is drunkenness just as bad? Apparently, it is.

And then there is the rest of the verse. Those who practice drunkenness will not inherit the kingdom of God. Really? If I continually practice drunkenness, I will not receive my inheritance? Kind of puts it on the line, doesn't it?

From what I see in this scripture, we can live lives of drunkenness and not have our inheritance, or we can abstain from drunkenness and receive our inheritance. I do not see choice number three. Do you?

What God Says about Sin

God's Word tells us that others may not know about our sin, but - He does. For God knows our very thought.

> He who planted the ear, shall He not hear?
> He who formed the eye, shall He not see?
> He who instructs the nations, shall He not correct. He who teaches man knowledge?
> The LORD knows the thoughts of man, that they are futile. (Psalm 94:9–11 NKJV)

God's Word also tells us that Jesus died because of our sin. Your sin. My sin.

> But God demonstrates His own love toward us, in that while we were still sinners, Christ died for us. (Romans 5:8 NKJV)

God tells us that we are to confess our sins to one another and pray for each other.

> Confess your trespasses to one another, and pray for one another, that you may be healed. The effective, fervent prayer or a righteous man avails much. (James 5:16 NKJV)

And Jesus Himself tells us that if our Christian brother sins against us we are not to go around telling others. We are to go to him alone and tell him.

"Moreover if your brother sins against you, go and tell him his fault between you and him alone. If he hears you, you have gained your brother." (Matthew 18: 15 NJKV)

We are not to judge others because they sin. Nor are to judge the sin they struggle with. Their struggles may or may not be the same struggles that we are dealing with. But it is their struggle all the same. Nor are we to judge how they do or do not deal with their sins. Instead, we are to uplift them and to encourage them. We are to help them. We are to be tender toward them and to forgive them no matter their sin.

Be kind to one another, tenderhearted, forgiving one another, even as God in Christ forgave you. (Ephesians 4:32 NKJV)

But we are warned not to confess our sins to just anyone. We are to be careful about whom we confide in. The people we go to should be mature Christians only. For those who are not Christians do not belong to God. And because they do not belong to God, they are not able to understand the things of God. Thus, they are not able to relate to our situation or to give us godly advice.

And they need to be Christians who are mature in God's Word. They need to not only know God's Word intimately, but how to apply it to life properly. God's Word tells us this.

Now we have received, not the spirit of the world, but the Spirit who is from God, that we might know the things that have been freely given to us by God. These things we also speak, not in words which man's wisdom teaches but which the Holy Spirit teaches, comparing spiritual things with spiritual.

But the natural man does not receive the things of the Spirit of God, for they are foolishness to him; nor can he know them, because they are spiritually discerned. (1 Corinthians 2:12–14 NKJV)

What Should I Know about Jesus Christ, the Lord?

What should I know about Jesus Christ? First and foremost, I need to know that Jesus Christ went to the cross and laid His life down to be my sacrificial sin Lamb. And He did so willingly.

> For Christ died for sins once for all, the righteous for the unrighteous, to bring you to God. He was put to death in the body but made alive by the Spirit, through whom also he went and preached to the spirits in prison who disobeyed long ago when God waited patiently in the days of Noah while the ark was being built. In it only a few people, eight in all, were saved through water, and this water symbolizes baptism that now saves you also—not the removal of dirt from the body but the pledge of a good conscience toward God. It saves you by the resurrection of Jesus Christ, who has gone into heaven and is at God's right hand—with angels, authorities, and powers in submission to him. (1 Peter 3:18-22 NIV)

But not just for me. He died for everyone's sin. For everyone who has lived, is living, and will live. And He died for all our sins. For everyone's sin. And not just the ones we do on accident or those we do in public, but for the ones we do on purpose. The ones we do in private. He died for those sins as well.

As God's Son, Jesus Christ was righteous while we are not. We are descendants of Adam and Eve, and we know what they did in the garden. They sinned and became unrighteous. Unless we have the blood of Jesus Christ on us, unless Jesus's blood has washed us clean of our sins, we still appear as unrighteousness to God.

Jesus went to the cross willingly. He told us so.

> "The reason my Father love me is that I lay down my life—only to take it up again. No one takes it from me, but I lay it down of my own accord. I have authority to lay it down and authority to take it up again. This command I received from my Father." (John 10:17–18 NIV)

Yes. Willingly. The night He was arrested, He had spent hours praying to His heavenly Father asking for the Father's release from the upcoming event. When the heavenly Father did not release Jesus, Jesus relented His will to the Father's will and said, "Not my will—but yours."

> Then Jesus went with his disciples to a place called Gethsemane, and he said to them, "Sit here while I go over there and pray." He took Peter and the two sons of Zebedee along with him, and he began to be sorrowful and troubled. Then he said to them, "My soul is overwhelmed with sorrow to the point of death. Stay here and keep watch with me."

Going a little farther, he fell with his face to the ground and prayed, "My Father, if it is possible, may this cup be taken from me. Yet not as I will, but as you will." (Matthew 26:36–39 NIV)

Jesus came to earth to live and die on the cross so we would not be condemned to an eternal life separate from God. Jesus gave us the ability to be saved from the condemnation of our sins. Which allows us to live in heaven with God and with Him.

God so loved the world that he gave his one and only Son, that whoever believes in him shall not perish but have eternal life. For God did not send his Son into the world to condemn the world, but to save the word through him. (John 3:16–17 NIV)

Jesus Christ is now the Lord of my life, which means He is my teacher, leader, and my shepherd – my good Shepherd - as well as my Savior. And as such He leads me down the paths I am to go. His relationship with me is intimate. He willingly dies for me. And - I am in His hand – forever. Jesus Himself told me so:

"I am the good shepherd. The good shepherd lays down his life for the sheep." (John 10:11 NIV)

"I am the good shepherd; I know my sheep and my sheep know me—just as the Father knows me and I know the Father—and I lay down my life for the sheep." (John 10:14–15 NIV)

"My sheep listen to my voice; I know them, and they follow me. I give them eternal life, and they shall never perish; no one can snatch them out of my hand. My Father, who has given them to me, is greater than all; no one can snatch them out of my Father's hand. I and the Father are one." (John 10:27–30 NIV)

God wanted to spend eternity with us so much that He asked His Son to come to earth in human form, live among us, and teach us what God wanted us to know and then to go to a cross to be crucified as our sacrificial guilt offering.

Jesus is my way – my only way - to the heavenly Father. That is what I need to know about Jesus.

Because of Jesus's Blood:

I am redeemed through Jesus Christ, my sacrificial sin Lamb.

> The next day John saw Jesus coming toward him and said, "Look, the Lamb of God, who takes away the sins of the world!" (John 1:29 NIV)

I have remission of sins through the blood of Jesus Christ.

> In him we have redemption through his blood, the forgiveness of sins, in accordance with the riches of God's grace that he lavished on us with all wisdom and understanding. (Ephesians 1:7–8 NIV)

I am now justified.

> Since we have now been justified by his blood, how much more shall we be saved from God's wrath through him! (Romans 5:9 NIV)

I have been reconciled to God.

> For if, when we were God's enemies, we were reconciled to him through the death of His Son, how much more, having been reconciled, shall we be saved through his

life! Not only is this so, but we also rejoice in God through our Lord Jesus Christ, through whom we have now received reconciliation. (Romans 5:10–11 NIV)

I now have peace, Jesus's peace.

Therefore, since we have been justified through faith, we have peace with God through our Lord Jesus Christ, through whom we have gained access by faith into this grace in which we now stand. And we rejoice in the glory of God. (Romans 5:1–2 NIV)

Be Careful of Vows

Then the Spirit of the LORD came upon Jephthah. He crossed Gilead and Manasseh, passed through Mizpah of Gilead, and from there he advanced against the Ammonites. And Jephthah made a vow to the LORD: "If you give the Ammonites into my hands, whatever comes out of the door of my house to meet me when I return in triumph from the Ammonites will be the LORD's, and I will sacrifice it as a burnt offering." (Judges 11:29–30 NIV)

When Jephthah returned to his home in Mizpah, who should come out to meet him but his daughter, dancing to the sound of tambourines! She was an only child. Except for her he had neither son nor daughter. When he saw her, he tore his clothes and cried, "Oh! My daughter! You have made me miserable and wretched, because I have made a vow to the LORD that I cannot break." (Judges 11:34–35 NIV)

Wow! Poor Jephthah! God has told us at least three to be careful when we make vows. Especially vows to Him.

Moses said to the heads of the tribes of Israel: "This is what the LORD commands: When a man makes a vow to the LORD or takes an oath to obligate himself by a pledge, he must not break his word but must do everything he said." (Numbers 30:1-2 NIV)

If you make a vow to the LORD your God, do not be slow to pay it, for the LORD your God will certainly demand it of you and you will be guilty of sin. But if you refrain from making a vow, you will not be guilty. Whatever your lips utter you must be sure to do, because you make your vow freely to the LORD your God with you own mouth. (Deuteronomy 23:21–23 NIV)

When you make a vow to God, do not delay in fulfilling it. He has no pleasure in fools; fulfill your vow. It is better not to vow than to make a vow and not fulfill it. Do not let your mouth lead you into sin. And do not protest to the temple messenger, "My vow was a mistake." Why should God be angry at what you say and destroy the work of your hands? Much dreaming and many words are meaningless. Therefore stand in awe of God. (Ecclesiastes 5:4–7 NIV)

When Jephthah made his vow to the Lord, I am quite sure that he never dreamed that it would be his one and only offspring, his daughter, who would be the promised sacrifice. The promised burnt offering. How his heart must have dropped to his feet when he saw his daughter coming through the doorway. I am sure all his being wanted to yell, "No! My daughter! Do not come out! Do not walk through the doorway!"

And yet, his daughter came out to greet her father dancing to music. One translation says she went to meet her father with tambourines. Can you not see this in your mind's eye? A daughter dancing with joy while she played on the tambourine because her father has come home.

Yet, Jephthah had made a vow to God - a promise, and he had to keep it. Not to do so would have been a broken vow to God – a sin. So, Jephthah had a decision. Which was he going to honor? His daughter's life or his vow to the Lord? How heart-wrenching! Remember this was just any daughter but his one and only daughter. In fact, she was his one and only child.

Again, we see that God's Word is true. And we see that God's warnings to us are for our own good. If we heed His warnings, our lives will be much better!

But that is not all we see in this scripture. We see Jephthah's daughter agreeing to do what her father asks her to do even though it might have caused her death.

> "My father," she replied, "you have given your word to the LORD. Do to me just as your promised, now that the LORD has avenged you of your enemies, the Ammonites."
> (Judges 11:35-36 NIV)

Who else did the same thing? Who agreed to do as His Father wished even though He knew it would cost Him His life? Jesus. Just like Jephthah God has only one offspring – Jesus. And just like Jephthah, God, the Almighty Heavenly Father sacrificed His one offspring. Sacrificed for my sins. For your sins.

As hard as I try, I cannot fully absorb the fact that Jesus loved me so much that He willingly laid down His life for me. That He willingly died a painful death on the cross. That He remained on the cross exposed for all to see until His death. And He this just so I could be viewed as righteous by God. That type of love is so far beyond my comprehension. And yet, that is how much Jesus loves me. Loves you.

And how much God loves even those who are not His – yet.

Desires of Your Heart

> Delight yourself also in the LORD, and He shall give you the Desires of your heart. (Psalm 37:4 NKJV)

For a long time, this scripture was a mystery to me. That was until I realized that it was not talking about God giving us the things we ask for, but about the condition of our hearts. God is interested in our hearts. Interested in the why we do the things we do. Or say the things we say. The motives behind our actions.

If our hearts are pure and we are seeking God and His wisdom, then our desires will parallel His. And if our hearts are filled with Gods Word—if Jesus is sitting on the throne of our hearts—then our hearts' desires will mirror His.

The Lord knows our hearts. He knows who the center of our life is. He knows who the lord of our life is. If it is the Alpha and the Omega, the big "G" God or if the center of our life is us, the little "g" god. Remember God knows the hearts of men.

God loves you and wants you to have the desires of your heart. But only if He is the center of your life. The Lord of your life. The Alpha and the Omega. The big "G" God. Only when God is all these things to us will we be able to desire the things of God with hearts that are pure. And only then will our motives be selfless, not selfish.

I'm not saying God will give us everything we ask for. I'm saying that when our hearts are filled with His Word, our hearts' desires will parallel His. We will no longer have a desire for things that are sinful or displeasing to Him. Our desire will be to do what pleases Him. Our desire will be to be obedient. To hear those words from our Lord's lips: "Thou good and faithful servant." And because of such, our desires will be for what a father—our heavenly Father—would want to give to His children.

Once our hearts are right, once we ask for desires from the Father for the right reasons, then He will give us those desires. And He just may bless our socks off.

How Crafty He Is

Last night, I watched a movie about a pastor who thought he had heard from God. When this pastor shared what he believed God had told him, it caused a great deal of controversy in his congregation and in the church's denomination nationwide. Now, I am not stating whether the pastor had really heard from God or not. I do not know for sure either way. Nor is this the subject of this article.

What is our subject is the fact that I saw a man who laid it all on the line for something he believed in. A man who stayed the course no matter what. I saw a man who did not waver from what he believed though many others were doubting him and even leaving him. I saw a man who was steadfast even when his mother, a woman of God, scolded him for what he believed.

I saw a man who lost all of his earthly wealth and comfort for standing firm in something he believed. A man who did not compromise even when he was strongly advised to by his superiors to do so. A man who was broke and under great emotional pressure, never walked away from what he believed.

Can you say that you do that? Can you say that as a Christian, you are willing to lose everything because of what you believe? Are you willing to stay closer to your belief in the redeeming blood of Jesus Christ than you are to your friends? To your family? Will you give up your church or your comfy home for your belief in God and Jesus? Will you be able to resist the demands of your superiors to compromise what you believe? And then when you are emotionally broken, will you still be willing to stand up for your belief? Will you be able to stand on broken legs and declare your belief in God and Jesus Christ?

Please my dear readers, there is not judgment here. For I am not asking these questions for answers, but for reflection. I cannot in all honesty say I could do such things. That all of my answers would be yes.

I saw something else as well. I saw a church that took what God had said about false teachers and false preachers seriously. A church that showed great respect for God's Word and was very careful to teach His Word properly. A church that realized how great a responsibility teaching God's Word was. A church that took God's warning about the mishandling of His Word seriously.

I saw a church rejecting someone who was not teaching what he should have been teaching. A congregation that was not afraid to keep God's Word pure. A congregation that took the last verses of Revelation seriously.

> For I testify to everyone who hears the words of the prophecy of this book: If anyone adds to these things, God will add to him the plagues that are written in this book; and if anyone takes away from the words of the book of this prophecy, God shall take away his part from the Book of Life, from the holy city, and from the things which are written in this book. (Revelation 22:18–19 NKJV)

But I think the most important thing that I saw in this movie was the insight of how stealthy and crafty Satan can be. How he can take down someone who is in a church leadership role. How Satan will, and does, takes God's

Word out of context. How Satan will distort Scripture. How he will use it for his benefit and not God's.

And - it brought to life God's Words in Ephesians.

> Finally, my brethren, be strong in the Lord and in the power of His might. Put on the shole armor of God, that you may be able to stand against the wiles of the devil. (Ephesians 6:10–11 NKJV)

The Storm

> On the same day, when evening had come, He said to them, "Let us cross over to the other side." Now when they had left the multitude, they took Him along in the boat as he was. And other little boats were also with Him.

> And a great windstorm arose, and the waves beat into the boat, so that it was already filling. But He was in the stern, asleep on a pillow. And they awoke Him and said to Him, "Teacher, do You not care that we are perishing?"

> Then He arose and rebuked the wind, and said to the sea, "Peace, be still!" And the wind ceased and there was a great calm. (Mark 4:35–39 NKJV)

Have I ever been in that boat with the disciples! There they were traveling down the path laid out for them by Jesus and along comes a storm. A windstorm that was so great it was threatening to capsize their boat. Can you imagine just how unnerving that must have been? You're being tossed around violently and hanging onto anything you can so to not be thrown overboard. The strong wind is making it difficult to converse with your fellow disciples. Strong waves are spilling over into your boat causing it to fill with water. "Surely this is the day I will die" are your thoughts.

Finally, when you have come to the end of your strength and you find your fear is almost more than you can stand, you go to Jesus for His help. You awake Him and in a voice that trembles you say these words, "Lord, we're dying here. Do you not care?"

I've been there. More than once. Haven't you? There have been times when I was happily walking the path the Lord has laid out before me when *Boom!* There it is. A huge and fierce storm. A raging storm. With winds that are so strong I can barely hang on. And rain that is so hard it not only stings my face but is filling my boat with water faster than I can bail. And, as if that is not enough, I feel as though I am in this storm alone. The strong winds are so loud I cannot converse with my fellow believers. And sad to say, I even feel as if Jesus has left me to fend for myself. Arg!

When the disciples found that they could not handle the storm in their own strength, they turned to Jesus for His help. For His strength. When they did so, and only when they did so, Jesus stood up and did something the disciples could never do. Something that only He could do. He spoke to the seas and calmed the storm.

Every time I do as the disciples in the boat did—turn to Jesus and ask Him to help me—Jesus stands up and either calms my storm or gives me the strength to hang on during my storm. Either way, every time I go to Jesus for help – every time - He is there, and He helps me. Every time – period.

Now let us look at something that may have gone unnoticed in this scripture. There are other little boats that are crossing to the other side with Jesus and His disciples.

They too, were also caught up in that raging storm. And even though Jesus was not in their boats, they also reaped the blessing of Jesus's calming the seas. *Hmmm.*

Now this fact raises an interesting question. Could it be that others may reap from the blessings that occur when we—you and I—reach the end of our strength and turn to Jesus for His strength? As my old friend would say – chew on that.

Zero Worry Allowed

Ever wonder why God tells us not to worry?

> For I, the LORD your God, will hold your
> right hand. Saying to you, "Fear not, I will
> help you." (Isaiah 41:13 NKJV)

Or Jesus Himself in His own words tells us not to fear?

> "Peace I leave with you, My peace I give to
> you; not as the world gives do I give to you.
> Let not your heart be troubled, neither let it
> be afraid." (John 14:27 NKJV)

Because - worry is not from God.

> For God has not given us a spirit of fear, but
> of power and of love and of a sound mind.
> (2 Timothy 1:7 NKJV)

So - if worry is not from God, it must be from Satan.
God and Satan are the only two choices we have here.
There is no third choice. So, having settled that, let us look
at how Satan uses worry to cause us problems.

1. Worry causes you to shut down. It causes your fight-
    or-flight response to kick in. Your decisions become
    nothing more than knee-jerk reactions. You tend to
    overreact or not react at all. You cannot concentrate
    or be creative.

2. Worry takes away your ability to hear. You cannot hear the advice of others. And you most surely cannot hear the voice of God. It is almost as if worry causes temporary deafness.
3. Worry causes negative feelings that can lead to a lack of trust in anyone and anything, God included.
4. Worry causes you to try to control your situation. Worry is bred from a feeling of losing control over a situation.
5. Worry causes you to hold on tightly to anything you can. It seems to disable your ability to let go and let God handle the situation.
6. Worry breeds doubt about God. Not about if God can, but if God *will.*
7. Worry has a way of creeping into your life. All areas of your life. I have been in churches where the leadership was so worried about what the congregation would think of the service that there was no room for the Holy Spirit. No room in the inn for Jesus. No space for God. How sad.

Since worry is something, I deal with myself, I have found a secret I want to share with you. When you are in a season of worry, put aside a designated daily hour for worry time. Yes. Worry time. A time when you are allowed to worry about all the worrisome situations in your life. And do not forget about those what ifs. Worry about them as well.

You are not allowed to worry at any time during the day except during your designated worry time. So should you find that you are starting to worry, stop and tell yourself,

No, not now. I can worry about this today at six. Then to make sure you don't forget what to worry about, write it down.

Always start your worry time with prayer even if it's nothing more than, "Oh my Heavenly Father, I'm so worried." End it with a time of thanksgiving. Make a list of at least ten things God has given you. Then thank Him for each and every item that is on your list. There is nothing too small or too large for your list. There was a time when my list contained such things as toothpaste, jeans, a bed to sleep in, and food. But I wrote them down and thank Him for them.

Be sure to thank Jesus for the ability to go to God in prayer. Thank Him for His obedience to the Cross. And thank your Heavenly Father for giving you His One and Only Son to be your sacrificial Lamb.

As you continue this daily ritual of designated worry time, a strange thing will happen. Your list of things you are thankful will become longer than your worry list. And your worry time will evolve into a time of prayer and quietness with the Lord. And you will find that your designated time of worry has now become your designated time of letting go and of prayer. And when worry tries to creep into your day, you will now say, "Thank you, Lord, for taking this worry from me." For instead of hanging onto your worries, you are now letting them go by placing them into God's hands.

Hmmm. Funny how that works.

The Guitar

My church is renting a church building. In the room that is now designated as the children's church was an old guitar thrown up on a file cabinet almost out of reach. I asked one of our leaders if he could ask the landlord how much they wanted for the guitar. And to my pleasant surprise, they said I could have it.

It had been some time since anyone had strummed this guitar, so it needed some TLC and new strings. My friend's son is a wiz at guitar repairs and offered to do the work for me. He worked on the guitar for about three weeks. When the guitar came home, I did not recognize it. The son had cleaned it up, replaced broken and worn parts, and put new strings on it. He smiled as he handed the guitar to me and asked me to strum it. And when it did, wow! It emitted a wonderful, resonating sound. Who knew that this old guitar formerly in need of repairs would sound like that!

We did discover one flaw in the guitar, a crack in its neck. Someone had broken it, *and* someone had repaired it. The repair was so finely done that you could see the fracture line *only when* the guitar was held up to the light at just the right angle. This guitar that had suffered a great accident, had been made new and now once again can be used.

Hmmm. Sound like someone you know?

When we accept God's gift of salvation through His Son Jesus Christ, we have accepted Jesus as our Sacrificial Lamb. We have asked Him to save us from our sins. Not just today's sins, but our past sins and our future sins. We have put ourselves in the hands of the one – the only one - who can clean us up, repair our cracks, and restore the righteousness that God yearns for us to have. He is the only one who can make us once again wonderful instruments that He can use. And will use.

> For by grace you have been saved through faith, and that not of yourselves; it is the gift of God, not of works, lest anyone should boast. For we are His workmanship, created in Christ Jesus for good works, which God prepared beforehand that we should walk in them. (Ephesians 2:8–10 (NKJV)

Thank you, Jesus for dying for us. We love you.

David The Shepherd

The LORD is my shepherd I shall not want. He makes me to lie down in green pastures; He leads me beside the still waters, He restores my soul; He leads me in the paths of righteousness for His name's sake. Yea, though I walk through the valley of the shadow of death, I will fear no evil; for You *are* with me; Your rod and Your staff, they comfort me. (Psalm 23:1–4 NKJV)

David penned a lot about God being his shepherd. Perhaps he did so because he had been a shepherd and was familiar with the concept of being one. David knew how much a shepherd cared for his sheep. And how much care sheep took. He knew how the shepherd would work relentlessly to protect and provide for them. How the shepherd would lead his sheep to a place where there was water, food, and rest. How the shepherd would know his sheep as a mother would her children. He would know what they were afraid of. What they found calming. What they liked. He would know the sound of their voices and they would know his.

God, through His Son Jesus, does the same for us – His sheep. He cares for us. Protects us. Provides for us. He leads us to both physical and spiritual food: to well water and Living Water. He knows us intimately. In fact, He knows us better than we know ourselves. He knows our fears. He knows how to calm us. He knows our likes and our dislikes. He knows our needs. Our desires. He knows the sound of our voices. And we know the sound of His.

So, David was right in using the shepherd concept. Jesus Christ Himself told us in His words that He is our Shepherd. Not just any shepherd – the good shepherd.

> "I am the good shepherd. The good shepherd gives His life for the sheep". (John 10:11 NKJV)

The Power of Music

For years, I have had a desire to do music in some manner. My voice is nowhere near that of an opera singer, but I love to sing, and I love to play instruments. When others sing to the songs I play, it is as though God has opened the floodgate of blessings. So, I search for new songs. Practice different tempos. Come up with new arrangements of old favorites. I love making music. The first time someone referred to me as a musician, I was taken aback.

Music is magical. It stirs souls. Soothes pain. Enhances worship. As a child, I played my records as loudly as my parents would allow so I could feel the music way down inside me. Music moves. Music creates memories. And it has a way of imprinting words, be they good or bad words, in our memories. Just play a few songs you listened to in high school. Remember the words? Of course you do.

Music sticks with us. It places deep and lasting notches in our minds and in our souls. Satan uses this power of music to teach anyone who listens to his music his ways. Especially our young. Satan will put lyrics to a catchy tune that reeks of violence, sexual immorality, and all sorts of evilness. People, especially our young, find themselves caught up in tunes that are fun. Singing words that talk about things they should not even know about. After repeatedly singing these songs, they begin to think that although the words of these songs may not be what they would sing in church, they are really not *all* that bad. After all they are just words.

Not that bad? Really? Remember who penned those words? Satan. Yes, I know. These songs were put together by people, but if these people do not belong to God and are not doing the work of God, by default, they belong to Satan and are doing Satan's work. Remember? It is God or Satan. No third choice here, folks.

So once again, we see Satan subtly encroaching on the lives of others and they are not aware of it. We see Satan using snappy tunes to encourage our young to sing his words. To learn his ways instead of God's ways. Satan knows the powerful impact that music has on our minds and on our souls. He knows how words put to music permeates us. So, he uses it.

Those who lead God's people in worship with songs are on the frontlines of spiritual warfare. I see them as the soldiers going out on a battlefield to scout the enemy so the rest of the platoon can safely enter it. They are stepping all over Satan's backyard when they lift up their voices to worship the Lord and our Savior in song and lead God's children to do the same.

God loves to hear his children worship Him with song. No matter how they sound. After all, He gave us our voices and wants us to sound the way we do. So, my Christian friend, lift up that voice of yours. Sing strong. Worship God with your voice in song. Sing His praises as loudly as you can. Let the Lord and His Son, Jesus, know just how much you love them. Sing!

And let us teach our young to do the same. Teach them to sing praise to the Lord and to His Son, Jesus Christ. In doing so, you will show them how to worship. And you will give them an alternative to Satan's music. Now that's a win-win.

Rejoice in the LORD, O you righteous! For praise from the upright is beautiful. Praise the LORD with the harp; make melody to Him with an instrument of ten strings. Sing to Him a new song; play skillfully with a shout of joy. (Psalm 33:1–3 NKJV)

A News Article

Turning on the evening news, there could have been a news article that went something like this.

As a man and his wife were leaving a food establishment, a man with a gun approached them yelling obscenities. The man pointed the gun at the couple and shot them multiple times. He then turned his gun on those on the street who were running away trying to escape. Then the man disappeared in the night.

Police are now looking for the assailant going door to door in the neighborhood asking for details of what happened. The police think this is a random act. And are asking why someone would commit such a senseless act.

Those who are not God's children would probably agree with the reporter and the police. For they were wondering why someone would do such a thing. *Why are people so violent? How could someone be so cruel?*

As the night went on the were several news breaks delivering up to date details. Those who were watching were probably sitting in fear. They would continue monitoring the TV for more information. For any new details. They might even lock their doors and turn on all the lights in their homes.

Watching the same news, God's children would understand why this man did such horrific acts. They would understand that Satan tells his children what to do. That those who belong to Satan are performing satanic acts. And that these acts, this violent nature of man, must come to pass. Scriptures tell us that in the end times, there will be great violence in the land. They will know that this is just another sign that Jesus will be coming back soon.

Yes, God's children will also lock their doors. And yes, they will also be fearful. But they will turn to Jesus and to their heavenly Father asking them to keep them safe. They will look to them for their comfort. And will trust in their protection.

> He who dwells in the secret place of the Most High shall abide under the shadow of the Almighty. I will say of the LORD, "He is my refuge and my fortress; My God, in Him I will trust." (Psalm 91:1–2 NKJV)

The Prince of the Power of the Air

God's Word tells us that Satan is the spirit who works in the sons of disobedience. The spirit who works in the lives of those who yield to their flesh.

> And you He made alive, who were dead in trespasses and sins, in which you once walked according to the course of this world, according to the prince of the power of the air, the spirit who now works in the sons of disobedience, among whom also we all once conducted ourselves in the lusts of our flesh, fulfilling the desires of the flesh and of the mind, and were by nature children of wrath, just as the others. (Ephesians 2:1–3 NKJV)

Satan keeps his children in the dark. He sticks his fingers in their ears and covers their eyes with his hands. He fears that should they see the light, should they hear the gospel and understand it, they would no longer be his sons of disobedience but would be the sons of God.

> But even if our gospel is veiled; it is veiled to those who are perishing, whose minds the god of this age has blinded, who do not believe, lest the light of the gospel of the glory of Christ, who is the image of God, should shine on them. (2 Corinthians 4:3–4 NKJV)

I had never thought of Satan as a spirit. I had always thought of him as some evil thing that traveled around looking for someone to devour. Someone who made it his life's mission to destroy men. As many as he could. Genesis tells us that man was made in the image of God, and since Satan does not like God, we can safely say that Satan does not like man.

It is as if Satan does not want to be alone with just his demons, so he is trying to take down as many men as he can. Or maybe he is trying to outdo God. Trying to have more souls on his side of the playing board. As though he is trying to see who can have the greatest number of children? Or which one can be the fullest, Heaven or hell.

Maybe he is trying to show God just who is the strongest. Flexing his spiritual muscles. Remember Satan was expelled from Heaven because he wants to be God. He wants to be just as strong as God. Just as powerful. That is why he was thrown out of heaven. Satan wanted a throne that was higher than God's.

> How you are fallen from heaven, O Lucifer, son of the morning! How you are cut down to the ground, you who weakened the nations! For you have said in your heart: "I will ascend into heaven, I will exalt my throne above the stars of God; I will also sit on the mount of the congregation on the farthest sides of the north; I will ascend above the heights of the clouds, I will be like the Most High." Yet you shall be brought down to Sheol, to the lowest depths of the pit. (Isaiah 14:12–15 NKJV)

David

I love David. He was a man who committed adultery and murder and yet God called him a man after His own heart because he was obedient.

> After removing Saul, he made David their king. He testified concerning him: "I have found David son of Jesse a man after my own heart; he will do everything I want him to do." (Acts 13:22 NIV)

David was willing to do as the Lord asked of him. David would consult with God for guidance before he went into battle. And then he would do what the Lord told him to do. He would fight when God said fight. Not fight when God said not to fight. And he would fight in the way that God said he should do. Then David would do something really special. He would ask the Lord what he was to do after the battle had been won.

> Now the Philistines had come and raided the Valley of Rephaim; so David inquired of God: "Shall I go and attack the Philistines? Will you hand them over to me?" The LORD answered him, "Go, I will hand them over to you." (1 Chronicles 14:9–10 NIV)

Just a few lines down, you will once again find David seeking guidance from the Lord and following it to the letter.

Once more the Philistines raided the valley; so David inquired of God again, and God answered him, "Do not go straight up, but circle around them and attack them in front of the balsam trees. As soon as you hear the sound of marching in the tops of the balsam trees, move out to battle, because that will mean God has gone out in front of you to strike the Philistine army." So David did as God commanded him, and they struck down the Philistine army, all the way from Gibeon to Gezer. So David's fame spread throughout every land, and the LORD made all the nations fear him. (1 Chronicles 14:13–17 NIV)

In this scripture, we find David following the Lord's instructions and the Lord preparing the way for David.

Some say the Bible is not true. That the Bible is just a good read. But what we have just looked at debunks that theory. Every good Bible teacher I have sat under has told me that scripture will prove itself. You will always find another scripture that will sustain the scripture you are studying. And this is just what we have found here.

Commit to the LORD whatever you do, and your plans will succeed. (Proverbs 16:3 NIV)

Scripture has told us that God found favor with David. We have just read how David would ask of the Lord before going into battle, and then he followed through on the plans God gave him. And look at how successful he was.

God's Word is true. What God tells us in the Bible is the

truth. 100% truth. And - Bible is <u>not</u> just a good read. No. It is our owner's manual for our lives. A manual given to us by God telling us how to live out our life. How to worship Him. How to treat others. And who His Son, Jesus Christ really is. Our Savior.

And through the stories found in the Bible such as David, we see how God is just. Loving. Merciful. How He guides us. Protects us. Loves us. And how He never, never breaks His promises. Thank You Lord.

Doubting and Fearing

"Do not be afraid for I Am with you," is what Jesus has told us for thousands of years. I can hear His voice telling me that today. And yet here I am, still living life with fear. Afraid of what the next day, the next hour, or even the next moment might bring. The loss of three loved ones. Increased responsibilities at work. A drastic change in my husband's work schedule. Major lifestyle changes. The emergency removal of my horse's eye. The call from my doctor with bad news.

All these events have occurred in the past ninety days, and they have taken a toll. They have chewed off a piece of my sanity. Left me skittish. Jumping physically at any sudden noise. Wondering *what next?*

Yes, Lord Jesus, I do hear Your voice. And I'm trying to be obedient. But oh, Lord, I am afraid. So afraid. Afraid of what this day may bring. Of the next disaster that is looming just off the horizon. And yet you tell me not to be. I am sorry for feeling this way. I want to know deep down in my heart that you will take care of me and keep me from harm. Please forgive me for having such feelings. For being afraid. For doubting You. For being so weak in my faith.

Ever feel that way? Feel this way today?

Fear causes us to not think right. To think askew. Fear will cause us to have difficulties making decisions. What if we should make the wrong one? Fear causes us to doubt the actions we should take. It causes us to do what we shouldn't do and not do what we should do. And fear causes us to overreact to stimuli that should be taken in stride. Why is fear such a strong emotion? Why does our heavenly Father tell us not to fear?

I wonder if maybe fear could be an outward sign that we are not fully trusting God. Or maybe an outward sign of our unbelief that God truly loves us and that He *will* truly care for us. Not necessarily unbelief that He can *but* that He *will. Hmmm.*

Maybe my fear is a sign of my immaturity or weak spiritual growth in an area that God will help me work on. If that is so, the only way for God to help me mature in this area is to place me in situations where He and He alone can help me. Ouch!

No matter which situation applies, fear is an open door for Satan to enter our minds and fill them with thoughts that substantiate our fears. Thoughts that will feed our doubts. He will sit on our shoulders and whisper in our ears lies like God does not really love us. Or maybe God will not rescue us this time.

And oh boy, will Satan have a heyday with such doubts. In the garden, he asked Eve just enough to cause her to doubt God's leadership in her life. Satan has used that tactic over and over because it works almost every time. God's Word warns us about Satan and his deceitful ways that could prove fatal. And we need to heed His warning.

> Therefore humble yourselves under the mighty hand of God, that He may exalt you in due time, casting all your care upon Him, for He cares for you. Be sober, be vigilant; because your adversary the devil walks about like a roaring lion, seeking whom he may devour. (1 Peter 5:6–8 NKJV)

Hold On Gently

Gently hold onto whatever God gives you. To do otherwise creates problems. You could shatter the things God has given to you by squeezing them too tightly. An example of this would be to overmanage what God has given you. When you try to do what God has given you to do in your strength, and not in His, you crowd out His strength. And anything not given room to grow will wither and die. Micromanagement can be a sign of either wanting to maintain control or a lack of trust in those you are working with. And in this case that would be God. Ouch!

Don't hold onto what God gives you with clenched hands. If you do should God want to replace the old with something new - or something better - before He can place that new, or better, into your hand, He will have to open your hand. And if it is clenched tightly in a fist, then He may have to pry it open one finger at a time. Which could be very painful. Can anyone say "Ouch"?

Five years ago, an accident took away my ability to ride and to show horses. But I did not want to let go of that part of my life. So, I held on. Held onto my saddles and my gear. Held onto my last show horse, Sonny. Held onto great expectations of riding and showing him.

Sonny was a gift that I firmly believe God had given me. He was a beautiful horse. He was large in size, bold and confident, yet obedient. A rich creamy-colored palomino who is bred for dressage, my preferred style of riding. He is my dream horse, and we had instantly bonded. So, I held on. And on. And on.

My doctors advised against riding unless I just sat on

the back and gently walked around. They were afraid that I would intensify my injuries should I fall off my horse. But I still held on. And on. And on.

After all, the same doctors had told me that I would always walk with a cane and a limp. However, by the grace of God, I am not. They told me that my injuries would not completely heal. That I would always have an area of missing tissue under a skin graft. Once again, by the grace of God, the tissue is slowly but surely returning. And they told me that because I had had five surgeries in a relatively short time, I would not regain feeling in the surgery site. But yes, you guessed it. By the grace of God, feeling is slowly but surely returning. So maybe they were wrong about the riding part. And so, I held on. And on. And on.

One afternoon as I was hosing down my beautiful show horse, a freakish accident happened. Sonny spooked at something in the nearby woods. Sonny, who is usually very bold, whirled around and prepared himself for flight. His sudden movement knocked me down onto my back. As he turned to run from the scary monster the lead rope wrapped around my finger. Sonny who was now running away from the monster, started dragging me around the yard by my ring finger. The faster Sonny dragged me across the yard, the more frightened he became. The more frightened he became, the faster he ran.

This scenario continued until Sonny finally just stopped. Not sure if he stopped because he was tired, or far enough from the monster, or his boldness returned. But the lack of forward movement allowed the lead rope to unravel itself from around my now broken finger. Not just a regular broken finger, but one that had to be surgically repaired.

Hmmm. Maybe the doctors were right that time. Maybe I should let go of my saddle and all of my gear. Let go of my great expectations of riding horses again. Let go of Sonny. Maybe I should listen.

While I was healing from surgery, I asked the Lord to help me find a home for my dream horse. He was such a nice horse, and I did not want him to go to just anyone. And since I felt that he was a gift from God, I felt that God needed to tell me where Sonny was to go. Where his next home should be.

A few days later, a young woman called to ask if my beautiful show horse was available. She had met Sonny a few years earlier and had fallen in love with him. She wanted him to be her personal horse.

After some time in prayer, I finally obeyed my Lord and consented to the sale. Letting go of Sonny may not have been the most difficult thing I have been asked to do, but it is extremely close. For once Sonny is gone, my dream of riding and showing him well be gone as well.

The lady showed up with a horse trailer that was a bit small for Sonny. He stood a true seventeen hands at the withers which is just under six feet tall. Horses like that require tall trailers. Sonny had not been loaded on one since the accident that had laid me up five years earlier. Which meant the smaller trailer could make loading him just a bit more difficult.

So, I asked the Lord for affirmation of His will. I asked, "Please Lord, if this is what you want, allow Sonny to quietly load up. Then I'll know for sure that I'm being obedient."

Within minutes, Sonny, along with his feed bucket and winter blanket were in the trailer and on their way. As I watched him standing in the trailer riding down the driveway of what used to be his home for the last time, I had to let go of him *and* my dreams of riding him ever again. It was as if Sonny was taking a part of my hopes and dreams with him. Extreme sadness filled my heart and tears flowed as I watched them drive away.

The Lord had removed something wonderful from my hand. From a clenched hand that He had to pry open. But the story does not end there.

Five years earlier while I was healing from multiple surgeries, I learned to play some musical instruments. There are not too many things you can do without walking or standing, but playing an instrument is one of them. And the Lord has used that ability for His work. Thank you, Lord.

But, because I had held onto a dream that I should have allowed to die, my left hand was in a cast. So, for a time, I was not only unable to ride horses, I was also unable to play music. All because I held on too tightly.

But the story does not end there either.

Once my finger healed, I needed therapy. My occupational therapist was very thorough and very attentive. She seemed to be interested in my lifestyle. She asked about what I liked and disliked. What were my hobbies. And which activities did I need to return to. During this time, she learned that I played violin, mandolin, and some guitar.

The day of my final therapy appointment came. The visit was to be my last if I was able to do everything asked of me. Not sure what to expect, I sat across from my therapist, who pulled out a violin from behind her desk and asked me to play it. I hesitated for a few moments. The only tunes I knew by heart were hymns, and I was in a very public place.

After a very short "Please, Lord, help me!" prayer, I

put the violin on my shoulder and started playing. After the first song, my therapist asked me to play three more. Halfway through the third piece, I became aware that others had entered the room. Finishing the song, I looked around and saw that the room was filled with therapists and patients. They were smiling and enjoying this mini concert. Everyone applauded my performance.

But the story doesn't end there either.

My therapist told me that I needed to play my guitar for a least thirty minutes a day to regain finger strength. Really? My therapy involves doing something I really enjoy every day. Wow.

God had to pry my hand open before He could remove the old—horses—and put in something new—music. And now I play these instruments as a form of worship to God. As a service to Him. Playing music connects my heart to God. It brings me great happiness and seems to do the same for others. And believe it or not, it is helping the broken dream part of my dreams to heal.

God's Word tells us that every good gift if from Him. Thank you, Lord, for such great gifts!

> Every good gift and every perfect gift is from above, and comes down from the Father of lights, with whom there is no variation or shadow of turning. (James 1:17 NKJV)

No Fake News Here

In recent years, we have been bombarded with what is called fake news, most of which is coming from the political arena. Some congressional leaders are opposing our president, and he is opposing congressional leaders. And in the middle is what has been referred to as fake news.

I am becoming very wary of all this battling. Unless we are expecting some bad tropical weather (I live in Florida), I no longer turn on the news. If there is fake news out there, how can I be sure that what I'm seeing on the news is the real news or the fake news?

But my friend, I know where you can find real news anytime. And this real news has all the markings of a great newscast. There are good stories about how someone has helped another. There are birth announcements. Stories of travel. Of battles won. War stories. Human interest stories. Stories of those who overcame unsurmountable odds and rose to high ranks in government.

Different authors—reporters—wrote these stories. All which are all true. No fake news here. No exaggeration. No embellishment. No added flair. Not even a small insertion of someone's opinion. They are all written as they occurred.

These stories are in the Bible. It's filled with wonderful stories. The Old and New Testament alike. You will find poetry and song lyrics in Psalms. Future- telling in Revelation. There is the Jacob and Esau story, which seems made for a movie. There are stories of wars. Stories of natural disasters. Of famines. Stories about good times and bad times. Love stories. Even stories that give that feel good ending like in Ruth.

You will find live accounts of Jesus's life. Of how He walked this earth teaching whoever would listen to Him. Healing those who needed healing. Feeding those who needed feeding. Scolding those who needed scolding. Casting out demons from those who were shackled by Satan's workers. The story of Jesus's time here would make a wonderful movie series or a multivolume novel. He did so much in His short time here with us. The most important thing we learn from the Bible is that Jesus was so loving that He gave His life for all. We can never fathom the extent of His love.

Are you looking for some real news? Some real help? Some real advice? You will find it in the Bible. And that my friend is the real- real news.

> All scripture is given by inspiration of God,
> and is profitable for doctrine, for reproof, for
> correction, for instruction in righteousness,
> that the man of God may be complete,
> thoroughly equipped for every good work.
> (2 Timothy 3:16–17 NKJV)

It's Christmas Time!

Christmas is the most wonderful time of the year. Time to decorate. Bake cookies. Wrap gifts. And watch Christmas programs. As I surf the channels looking for those programs, I find plenty of other programs depicting people celebrating Christmas the best way they know how. TV programs filled with people who seem to be searching what Christmas really is. They say that Christmas is being with family. Giving to the needy. It's the season of love and of caring for others. A season of giving and receiving. These programs also tell us to celebrate the season cheerfully.

And then there are the many Christmas parties given to help you celebrate. Parties filled with joking and laugher and merrymaking. Parties that Christians might not feel comfortable at.

During the Christmas season, we see an uptake in giving to the poor and needy. It is almost as if helping those who need a hand up is an actual Christmas tradition. I think this is a wonderful part of the Christmas season. And I think this is a part of Christmas that Jesus would like.

We have songs that tell us that Santa Claus is on his way with lots of toys for good little boys and girls. So, we hang stockings for him to fill. We are told that Santa has a supernatural power that gives him the ability to travel the entire world in one night. This enables Santa to make sure all the little boys and girls get gifts. We are also told that he knows who has been naughty or nice, which means he must be able to know the hearts of men.

Those who have not accepted Jesus Christ as their

Savior cannot truly understand what Christmas really is. What Christmas is really about. Unless you know Jesus as your Savior, you cannot fully understand and appreciate that Christmas is the time of the year when we celebrate the birth of Jesus Christ, who is the King of Kings, the Lord of Lords, the Messiah. Only Christians can fully understand that Jesus Christ *is* God's Son. That Jesus is the sacrificial sin Lamb for all people everywhere for all time. That it is Jesus who can travel the entire world in one night. And it is God and God alone who knows the hearts of men. Only God can truly know who has been naughty or nice. And only God can reward men.

> "I the LORD search the heart and examine the mind, to reward a man according to his conduct, according to what his deeds deserve." (Jeremiah 17:10 NIV)

Those who say Christmas is something else do not fully understand the reason for the Christmas season. And without their knowledge, they may be telling us which side of the fence they are on—God's or Satan's. As God's Word tells us, unless they know Jesus as their personal Savior, as their sacrificial sin Lamb, they cannot know the things of God and thus not understand how special Jesus's birth is. They cannot know the real reason for Christmas.

> But the natural man does not receive the things of the Spirit of God, for they are foolishness to him; nor can he know them, because they are spiritually discerned. (1 Corinthians 2:14 NKJV)

Israel Has Wonderitis

Yes, I know. Wonderitis is a made-up word. The editor part of the Word app is screaming at me. The red line under "wonderitis" tells me that I have a misspelled the word. But wonderitis is what I would like to talk about. Because God's chosen people, the Israelites, were full of this wonderitis.

They would run to God for His mercy and His blessings and then after they had enjoyed both for a while, they would turn from Him and run back to their idols and to their wayward living. The Old Testament is filled with this behavior. We read that Israel repeated this over and over. And how God as their heavenly Father would scold them for such behavior. They repented of their wayward behavior and run back to God. And God would take them back. Again, and again.

There was a time when God spoke of giving Israel her certificate of divorce because her behavior was so bad. God equated Israel's behavior with adultery. Can you not hear His broken heart in the following Scripture?

> The LORD said also to me in the days of Josiah the king: "Have you seen what backsliding Israel has done? She has gone up on every high mountain and under every green tree, and there played the harlot. And I said, after she had done all these things, 'Return to Me.' But she did not return. And her treacherous sister Judah saw it. Then I saw that for all the causes for which backsliding Israel had committed adultery, I

had put her away and given her a certificate of divorce; yet her treacherous sister Judah did not fear, but went and played the harlot also."

"So it came to pass, through her causal harlotry, that she defiled the land and committed adultery with stones and trees. And yet for all this her treacherous sister Judah has not turned to Me with her whole hear, but in pretense," says the LORD. (Jeremiah 3:6–9 NKJV)

God told the nation of Israel that He was her husband. And that although they had committed adultery with their idols of stone and wood, should they sincerely repent with their whole heart, He would no longer be angry with them. And with the gentleness of a heart that is filled with mercy and love, God calls His nation back to Him.

"Go and proclaim these words toward the north, and say: 'Return, backsliding Israel,' says the LORD; 'I will not cause My anger to fall on you. For I am merciful,' says the LORD; "I will not remain angry forever. Only acknowledge your iniquity, that you have transgressed against the LORD your God, and have scattered your charms to alien deities under every green tree, and you have not obeyed My voice,' says the LORD." (Jeremiah 3:12-13 NKJV)

In fact, He would bless them with leaders who would thirst for His heart and with leaders who would lead them with knowledge and understanding of His ways. God told them that they would become a nation known as Jerusalem, the throne of the Lord. God must have really love Israel.

> "Return, O backsliding children," says the LORD; "for I am married to you. I will take you, one from a city and two from a family, and I will bring you to Zion. And I will give you shepherds according to My heart, who will feed you with knowledge and understanding." (Jeremiah 3:14–15 NKJV)

> At that time Jerusalem shall be called The Throne of the LORD, and all the nations shall be gathered to it, to the name of the LORD, to Jerusalem. No more shall they follow the dictates of their evil hearts. (Jeremiah 3:17 NKJV)

God pleaded again for Israel to return to Him. Can you not hear the sadness and the pain of God's words?

> "But I said: 'How can I put you among the children and give you a pleasant land, a beautiful heritage of the hosts or nations?'"

> "And I said: 'You shall call Me, "My Father," and not turn away from Me.' Surely, as a wife treacherously departs from her husband, so have you dealt treacherously with Me, O house of Israel," says the LORD.

A voice was heard on the desolate heights,
weeping and supplications of the children
of Israel. For they have perverted their way;
they have forgotten the LORD their God.

"Return, you backsliding children, and I will
heal your backslidings."

"Indeed we do come to You, for You are the
LORD our God. (Jeremiah 3:19–22 NKJV)

Why could the people of Israel not see how much God
loved them? Why did they not hear how they had broken
God's heart? Why were they so slow to learn that God's
ways were the best? Why did they always go back to idols of
wood and stone when they had the almighty God?

But before we get all haughty and get in the faces of
the Israelites, let us step back and look at our lives. Our
behavior. I tend to do the same thing as the Israelites
did—run to God for His mercy and blessings and truly
enjoy them. For a while. And then I find myself slowly but
surely drifting from God and from His ways. I find myself
drifting back to me and my ways.

The drift is slow and soft and gentle. So much so that I
do not notice it. That is, until I have drifted far away. So far
that I have not read God's Word for days and am existing
on only popcorn prayers. I have allowed the cares of the
world to infiltrate my time with God and have not spent
good quality quiet time with God. For days. Sometimes
weeks. I have drifted back to life with my idols. Back to
relying on my strength not God's. Back to me-issm. Ouch!
I have now become an adulterous wife to God. I have
become like a harlot. Not my proudest behavior for sure.

So, if this can happen to me and to you with all of today's modern ways of hearing and studying God's Word, why not to the Israelites, who were having to live God's Word? To a nation that did not have a Bible in their language. Or a nation that was not able to listen to God's Word on their laptop or CD player or phone.

The best part of this entire article is that even if we push God to the point that He wants to divorce us, should we sincerely repent with our entire heart, God will forgive us. He will take us back and call us His children once again. And He will shower us with His blessings.

Thank you, Lord, for loving us so.

It's Party Time!

Throughout God's Word, we see that angels praise and worship God. One great example of this is when our Savior was born. Now we all know the story of Jesus's birth. How the angels visited the shepherds tending their sheep. How they celebrated the birth of Jesus. And how even the Heavenly Hosts celebrated.

Just imagine you are a shepherd out in a field near Bethlehem. Your flock of sheep have just settled in for the night. So, you do likewise. For the day had been quite busy and you are very tired. And then from nowhere comes a great light that is so bright it feels like the noon day. Squinting you make out an angel standing in front of you. This angel tells you that he is from God. That you are not to be afraid. For he has great news for you. The Messiah who you had so long waited for is now here. For He has just been born in a nearby stable. The angel tells you where to find and how to recognize the Messiah.

Then heavenly hosts appear. Not just one or two, but a multitude of hoses. More than you can count. And together in one great unison the multitude of hosts were saying, "Gory to God in the highest, and on earth peace, goodwill toward men!" You are watching the angels worship God! Their voices were angelic. Their joy was contagious. You watch in splendor as they praise and worship the Lord God Almighty.

And then just as quickly as they came – poof - they are gone. Everything is gone. The heavenly hosts. The angel. The bright light. Everything. Not sure that you really did see and hear what you think you saw and heard, you ask your fellow shepherds if they saw the same thing. And they had. So, as a group you and your fellow shepherds decide to go and see the newly born Messiah.

> And she brought forth her firstborn Son, and wrapped Him in Swaddling cloths, and laid Him in a manger, because there was no room for them in the inn. Now there were in the same country shepherds living out in the fields, keeping watch over their flock by night.

> And behold, an angel of the Lord stood before them, and the glory of the Lord shone around them, and they were greatly afraid. Then the angel said to them, "Do not be afraid, for behold, I bring you good tidings of great joy which will be to all people. For there is born to you this day in the city of David a Savior, who is Christ the Lord. And this will be the sign to you: You will find a Babe wrapped in swaddling cloths, lying in a manger."

> And suddenly there was with the angel a multitude of the heavenly host praising God and saying: "Gory to God in the highest, and on earth peace, goodwill toward men!"

> So it was, when the angels had gone away from them into heaven, that the shepherds said to one another, "Let us now go to Bethlehem and see this thing that has come

to pass, which the Lord has made known to us." (Luke 2:7–15 NKJV)

We are told that the angels praised and worshipped God. Did the heavenly hosts sing the words they told the shepherds? Scripture does not say. Since music is part of praising and worshipping, I can just see in my mind's eye a choir of heavenly hosts singing songs of praise in angelic voices. How could God not find that pleasing? And how could the angels and heavenly host not sing for Him?

Do you know that there is another time when we are told the angels praise and worship the Lord? Yes, there is. Every time someone accepts Jesus as their personal Savior, the very second Jesus becomes their atonement for their sins, the angels celebrate.

In the words of our Lord and Savior, Jesus Christ:

> "What man of you, having a hundred sheep, if he loses one of them, does not leave the ninety-nine in the wilderness and go after the one which is lost until he finds it? And when he has found it, he lays it on his shoulders, rejoicing. And when he comes home, he calls to together his friends and neighbors, saying to them, "Rejoice with me, for I have found my sheep which was lost!"

> "I say to you that likewise there will be more joy in heaven over one sinner who repents than over ninety-nine just persons who need no repentance."

"Or what woman, having ten silver coins, if she loses one coin, does not light a lamp, sweep the house and search carefully until she finds it? And when she has found it, she calls her friends and neighbors together, saying, "Rejoice with me, for I have found the piece which I lost!"

"Likewise, I say to you, there is joy in the presence of the angels of God over one sinner who repents." (Luke 15:4–10 NKJV)

There is more joy in heaven when one soul is saved by the saving blood of Jesus than for ninety-nine souls who have no need to repent. Any lost soul who has been washed cleaned by the Blood of Jesus is a reason for the angels to rejoice in Heaven. Souls that have repented of their wicked ways. Souls that are covered in the blood of Jesus. Souls that are now among His sheep. Souls that the Savior has looked all over the house for. Those souls.

Do Not Overwork?

> Do not overwork to be rich; because of your
> own understanding, cease! (Proverbs 23:4
> NKJV)

That is a powerful statement. And one that seems to
contradict another scripture.

> Bondservants, obey in all things your
> masters according to the flesh, not with
> eyeservice, as men-pleasers, but in sincerity
> of heart, fearing God. And whatever you do,
> do it heartily, as to the Lord and not to men,
> knowing that from the Lord you will receive
> the reward of the inheritance; for you serve
> the Lord Christ. (Colossians 3:22–24 NKJV)

See what I mean? We have one scripture telling us that
we are not too overwork and another telling us that we
should work as if the Lord were right there watching our
every move and listening to our every word. How could
this be?

I have learned from a wise old friend that if you have
any questions in life, scripture has the answer. Even in this
case.

> For he who is called in the Lord while a slave
> is the Lord's freedman. Likewise he who is
> called while free is Christ's slave. You were

bought at a price; do not become slaves of
men. (1 Corinthians 7:22–23 NKJV)

There's the answer to our question. God's Word tells us
that those of us who have been called by God are free from
any type of man's slavery for we are now His slaves. He paid
for us with the blood of His Son; thus, we belong to Him.

Since we are slaves or bondservants of God's, we are to
work for Him, for He is now our Master. We are not to be
man pleasers, but God pleasers. And we are not to worry
about what man thinks of us, but what God thinks of us.
For it is He who has enabled us to do the work that we are
doing for man. Not man. And as His bondservants, we are
to do that work well. In doing so, we honor Him and Jesus
Christ with our obedience.

Those who do not belong to God will see a difference
in us. We will look different because unbeknown to them,
they are seeing Jesus Christ through us. They see us working
hard, being honest, and treating others fairly. They see us
doing things that are a rarity in today's business world. So,
when we live out Colossians 3:22–24, we are telling others
about the Lord and Jesus Christ without saying a word.
Reminds me of another scripture that states that faith
without works is dead.

And that is not all. We are setting an example for those
around us in the workforce who are Christians. We may
be leading those who have strayed back to the throne of
God by our work ethics. They may have secretly strayed
from the Lord or have been ignoring Jesus's calling. They
may be brothers or sisters in Christ who have been secretly
suffering. And our actions and obedience could be just the
little nudge that they need.

Either way, by being obediently handling our work given to us by God in a manner that honors God, others can see that we are God's child. Which can open a door for them to approach us should they need to.

"Okay," you say. "I get that part. But what about the do not overwork part?" Let us see if scripture can once again help us with that.

> Trust in the LORD with all your heart, and lean not on your own understanding; in all your ways acknowledge Him, and He will make your paths straight. (Proverbs 3:5–6 NIV)

This scripture tells us to trust in the Lord with all our hearts. Not to trust in man. Not to trust in our employers. Not to trust in our government. But to trust in the Lord. And the Lord only. With all our hearts. With all our minds. And with all our souls. Not just part – but all.

If we are living as God has asked us to, we can trust God to take care of us. We can trust that God will direct our paths in ways that ensure we have what we need when we need it along with a desire or two on the side. Which means we will no longer have to overwork to gain those things, because we are trusting God to provide them. Thus, we can rest after a hard day's work. For we know that God is caring for us. God has told us He would. And God cannot lie.

Hmmm. I feel another scripture coming along. In Hebrews, Joshua was speaking to the people about God's rest.

There remains, then, a Sabbath-rest for the people of God; for anyone who enters God's rest also rests from his own work, just as God did from his. Let us, therefore, make every effort to enter that rest, so that no one will fall by following their example of disobedience. (Hebrews 4:9–11 NIV)

If resting in God's promise of provision, if resting in the arms of Jesus as my Savior is being obedient to God, then I am going to rest. Want to join me?

Standing at Crossroad

While standing at the crossroads of life, I agonized over which road to take. I have been traveling down the one to the right for some time. But I see the trail narrowing with a sharp turn not far away. I cannot see what is past the sharp curve.

There is the path on the left which is new to me. This path seems to be overtaken with vines and obstacles. Travel on this pathway will be difficult and shaky at best. So I stand at the crossroad, perplexed about which way to go. Unsure, I have worried and fretted almost to the point of physical affliction. Ever been there?

After spending time with my Bible this morning, I picked up my favorite devotional, found today's date, and read what it had to say. And you'll never believe what I read. The Lord was reminding me that He came to set me free. And that should I freely allow His Holy Spirit to lead my thoughts and my actions. That I am to focus on the Lord. Then I can do what He has laid before me to do. And—get this—as I follow Him down the new path, I need not worry about what is on the road ahead. I am to find security in Him, not in circumstances or the way things look.

Amazed at what I had just read, I closed the devotional and thanked God for His guidance. Isn't our Lord good? He sent Jesus Christ so we could have a way to talk with Him. A way to seek guidance from Him.

God answers all our questions. All of them. He does so through people, through sermons, through songs, and even through devotionals. Knowing this makes reading a daily devotional so to see how that day's reading applies to our questions fun and exciting.

It is comforting to know which way we are to go when standing at crossroads. That is why people seek answers. However, unlike those of us who turn to God and His Word for guidance, so many people turn to horoscopes or palm readers. Scripture tells us to stay away from such things, for they are not of God. Which means they must be of Satan. Remember, it is God <u>or</u> Satan—only two choices.

> "'Do not turn to mediums or seek out spiritists, for you will be defiled by them. I am the LORD your God.'" (Leviticus 19:31 NIV)

Unlike God, Satan is the great deceiver who looks for those he can devour. And he is deceiving a great many people who base their life decisions on horoscopes or palm readings. Once again, Satan is trying to imitate God and His ways. God leads with His Word while Satan leads with his horoscopes, palm readers, and the like. People will innocently seek out guidance from palm readers when facing some very important life decisions. They are not aware of whom they are consulting with. Scary!

Any time we go to Satan for advice we receive bad advice. Satan cannot tell us the truth about anything. Remember, Jesus told us that Satan's native language was lies. And if lies are Satan's native language, then Satan does not have the ability to speak the truth.

> "You belong to your father, the devil, and you want to carry out your father's desire. He was a murderer from the beginning, not

holding to the truth, for there is no truth in him. When he lies, he speaks his native language, for he is a liar and the father of lies." (John 8:44 NIV)

So, when Satan tells you things, either direct through whispering in your ear, or indirectly through palm readings, remember this is not the truth. If you want to know the truth, go to Jesus. For He is the truth and the light.

Whirlwind Season

Whew! I am tired. My life is in a whirlwind as I try to balance two part-time jobs with one of which needs at least full-time hours and then some. I quietly wondered if God feels that all of this work—that all of my busyness—is in vain. And I wonder, *Is it sinful?* God Himself rested on the seventh day. I'm sure God didn't rest because He was tired or was done with His work. He did it to set an example for us to follow.

During this whirlwind season, I've tried to get everything done by Saturday so I could rest on Sunday, but that requires self-discipline and strict time management considering my full-time (and then some) employment, music, work for my church, and writing. Add everyday stuff like grocery shopping, doctor appointments, and such and I am, busy!

But before I come down on myself too harshly, let us look at the work ethic of the Israelites. You know, during biblical times. Times when you laboriously grew your own fruits, grains, and vegetables and raised your own livestock for meat. When you had to gather wood for cooking. Thank you, Lord, for stoves!

While still in the desert, before they ever planted their first crops in the Promised Land, God gave His people ten guidelines He wanted them to follow. Today, we call them the Ten Commandments. Starting with the eighth commandment, God told His people that they were to rest on the seventh day of the week, the Sabbath.

Remember the Sabbath day by keeping it holy. Six days you shall labor and do all your work, but the seventh day is a sabbath to the LORD your God. On it you shall not do any work, neither you, nor your son, or daughter, nor your manservant or maidservant, nor your animals, nor the alien within your gates. For in six days the LORD made the heavens and the earth, the sea, and all that is in them, but he rested on the seventh day. Therefore the LORD blessed the Sabbath day and made it holy. (Exodus 20:8–11 NIV)

Even amid all this hard work, the Israelites obeyed God's command regarding their rest time. They made sure that their work was done by the end of the week, and they rested on the Sabbath. Without modern machinery and modern conveniences.

And then there was our Savior, Jesus, who ministered to thousands at a time. Healing and preaching. Feeding the poor. Giving sight to the blind. Yet we are told that there were times when Jesus would go off by Himself to rest and to spend time with the heavenly Father. Yes, my friend, another example of how we are to treat our work. Another example to teach us that though we are expected to work hard, we are also expected to take time for God. To take time to be with God. To rest in God.

Jesus is our example of this. He prayed on a mountain during the day.

After he had dismissed them, he went up on a mountain by himself to pray. (Matthew 14:22 NIV)

And we are to take time to talk with our Heavenly Father. Should we follow the lead of Jesus we are to get up early so to have time in prayer before our day starts. Even if it is before the sun comes up. Jesus did.

> Very early in the morning, while it was still dark, Jesus got up, left the house and sent off to a solitary place, where he prayed. (Mark 1:35 NIV)

We have found that we are not to place our work time about our God time. And our God time should be quiet times away from others. This will give us the ability to give God and Jesus our entire attention. And will enable us to hear their voice. To hear the things that God wants to tell us. To see the things that God wants to show us. And it will give us the ability to be with God and our Savior on a very intimate level. What a wonderful place to be – in the presence of God and His Son my Savior – Jesus. ☺

Do as the Pharisees Do?

Jesus told the Pharisees that they were not going to enter Heaven. In fact, Jesus also told the Pharisees that they were keeping the church from going to Heaven as well.

> 'Woe to you, teachers of the law and Pharisees, you hypocrites! You shut the kingdom of heaven in men's faces. You yourselves do not enter, nor will you let those enter who are trying to." (Matthew 23:13 NIV)

Jesus called the Pharisees the sons of hell. And told them that they are making their converts sons of hell as well.

> "Woe to you, teachers of the law and Pharisees, you hypocrites! You travel over land and sea to win a single convert, and when he becomes one, you make him twice as much a son of hell as you are." (Matthew 23:15 NIV)

But Jesus did not stop there; He called the Pharisees blind guides.

> "Woe to you blind guides! You say, "If anyone swears by the temple, it means nothing; but if anyone swears by the gold of the temple, he is bound by his oath." (Matthew 23:16 NIV)

And blind fools.

> "You blind fools! Which is greater; the gold,
> or the temple that makes the gold sacred?"
> (Matthew 23:17 NIV)

And whitewashed tombs.

> "Woe to you, teachers of the law and
> Pharisees, you hypocrites! You are like
> whitewashed tombs, which look beautiful
> on the outside but on the inside are full of
> dead men's bones and everything unclean.
> In the same way, on the outside you appear
> to people as righteous but on the inside
> you are full of hypocrisy and wickedness."
> (Matthew 23:27–28 NIV)

And then Jesus really poured it on calling the Pharisees a brood of venomous snakes – vipers who are condemned to hell!

> "You snakes! You brood of vipers! How
> will you escape being condemned to hell?"
> (Matthew 23:33 NIV)

Wow! What strong words! Why was Jesus so angry with the Pharisees? What caused Him to say such awful things to the Pharisees. Well, let us look at what was happening and see why Jesus said such things.

First off, we see that there were some among the Pharisees who were not as they seemed. They were false teachers who appeared to be more interested in looking good than being good.

> Then Jesus said to the crowds and to his disciples: "The teachers of the law and the Pharisees sit in Moses' seat. So you must obey them and do everything they tell you. but do not do what they do, for they do not practice what they preach. They tie up heavy loads and put them on men's shoulders, but they themselves are not willing to lift a finger to move them."
>
> Everything they do is done for men to see: They make their phylacteries wide and the tassels on their garments long; they love the place of honor at banquets and the most important seats in the synagogues; they love to be greeted in the marketplaces and to have men call them "Rabbi." (Matthew 23:1–7 NIV)

The Pharisees were more interested in themselves and in their reputations than they were in the members of their church. They loved the attention and special treatment that came with being Pharisees. The work they did for the church was not really for the church but was done to make them look good.

The Pharisees placed more emphasis on laws and the keeping of laws than they did on grace and mercy. They had loaded down the church members with a large number of dos and don'ts. They dared anyone to challenge them. And they neglected mercy. And Jesus called them on it.

"Woe to you, teachers of the law and Pharisees, you hypocrites! You give a tenth of your spices – mint, dill and cumin. But you have neglected the more important matters of the law – justice, mercy and faithfulness. You should have practiced the latter, without neglecting the former. You blind guides! You strain out a gnat but swallow a camel." (Matthew 23:23–24 NIV)

Jesus was upset with the Pharisees because they were the ones who were to minister to the church, teach scriptures, counsel, feed the hungry, care for the widows, and lead their congregants to a closer relationship with God.

Instead, they told the people to do one thing and did the opposite. They burdened the people with many laws and then watched to make sure the people obeyed each one of them.

The Pharisees wanted to appear spiritual. So, they made sure their phylacteries were wide and the tassels on their garments long. And they loved all the special treatment given to them as Pharisees.

Phylacteries are boxes that are sometimes filled with scriptures. Any Jewish male thirteen and older are to wear them. One box is worn on the head just atop the forehead, and another is worn of the upper left arm. The reasoning behind these boxes is the belief that the boxes help to make the men more spiritual, closer to God. The box on the head is a symbol of the wearer's mental emotions for God while the box on the arm is a symbol of the man's heartfelt emotions for God.

The Pharisees made sure that their boxes were wide;

they wanted all to see just how much heartfelt emotions they had for God and how great their mentality toward the Lord almighty was and how spiritual they were. Not the walk of a true teacher of God's Word. According to what we have just learned, the Pharisees as a whole were acting more like false teachers. Jesus told us that that the Pharisees did not practice what they preached.

> "The teachers of the law and the Pharisees sit in Moses' seat. So you must obey them and do everything they tell you. But do not do what they do, for they do not practice what they preach." (Matthew 23:2–3 NIV)

But what about today's Christian leaders who are acting as the Pharisees did? Who are not walking their talk just as the Pharisees did? Who put more emphasis on works and not so much on grace as the Pharisees did? Who are not listening to the teachings of Jesus Christ as the Pharisees did? Who are just as harmful to God's church as the Pharisees were? Who want us to see just how spiritual they are as the Pharisees did?

God has warned us that the closer we get to what Christians refer to as the end times, the more frequently false teachers will appear. God told us not to have anything to do with false teachers for their teachings are destructive. They will lead us away from the truth. Away from the Gospel. They are Satan's workers, masquerading as one of God's. And they may come from the church! From your church! Yes, even my church!

> But there were also false prophets among the people, just as there will be false teachers

among you. They will secretly introduce destructive heresies, even denying the sovereign Lord who bought them – bringing swift destruction on themselves. Many will follow their shameful ways and will bring the way of truth into disrepute. In their greed these teachers will exploit you with stories they have made up. Their condemnation has long been hanging over them, and their destruction has not been sleeping. (2 Peter 2:1–3 NIV)

For such men are false apostles, deceitful workmen, masquerading as apostles of Christ. And no wonder, for Satan himself masquerades as an angel of light. It is not surprising, then, if his servants masquerade as servants of righteousness. Their end will be what their actions deserve. (2 Corinthians 11:13–15 NIV)

How then are we to know if teachers are false teacher? Test them.

Dear friends, do not believe every spirit, but test the spirits to see whether they are from God, because many false prophets have gone out into the world. This is how you can recognize the Spirit of God: Every spirit that acknowledges that Jesus Christ has come in the flesh is from God, but every spirit that does not acknowledge Jesus is not from God. This is the spirit of the antichrist, which you have heard is coming and even now is already in the world. (1 John 4:1–3 NIV)

We have also been told to test their fruit to see if it is good or bad. How close to scripture are they staying in their teachings? Are they taking verses out of context? Are they using scripture to fit their sermons instead of making their sermons fit scripture? Are they using their ministry for their benefit? For their personal cause? Are they caring for their flock? Do they allow the Holy Spirit to guide them? What does the fruit in their live look like? Good or bad?

In the words of Jesus Christ,

> "Watch out for false prophets. They come to you in sheep's clothing, but inwardly they are ferocious wolves. By their fruit you will recognize them. Do people pick grapes from thornbushes, or figs from thistles? Likewise every good tree bears good fruit, but a bad tree bears bad fruit. A good tree cannot bear bad fruit, and a bad tree cannot bear good fruit. Every tree that does not bear good fruit is cut down and thrown into the fire. Thus, by their fruit you will recognize them." (Matthew 7:15–20 NIV)

Let us not be as the Pharisees were—pompous, prideful, and selfish. Let us be humble, gentle, and loving. Let us not walk around with really big phylacteries attached to our heads and arms, so that all can see just how religious we truly are. But let us live in a way that all can see just how precious Jesus is. Let us live a life that is reflective of our Savior.

Let us not be as false teachers who distort God's Word; let us always handle it in the proper manner. We are to treat the things of the Lord God almighty with the upmost respect and reverence. We are to not take His Word out of context or twist it to suit our needs. God takes such actions seriously. Need I remind you of what God says about those who mistreat His Word?

> I am astonished that you are so quickly deserting the one who called you by the grace of Christ and are turning to a different gospel – which is really no gospel at all. Evidently some people are throwing you into confusion and are trying to pervert the gospel of Christ. But even if we or an angel from heaven should preach a gospel other than the one we preached to you, let him be eternally condemned! As we have already said, so now I say again: If anybody is preaching to you a gospel other than what you accepted, let him be eternally condemned! (Galatians 1:6–9 NIV)

Yes. Those who do not handle God's Word correctly, those who are not teaching the true gospel, are condemned - eternally.

But that is not all God has to say about those who do not teach His Word correctly. He has a much greater warning for those who teach. Especially for those who teach false doctrine.

Not many of you should presume to be teachers, my brothers, because you know that we who teach will be judged more strictly. (James 3:1 NIV)

Ouch! May this stern warning sink into the hearts of anyone who teaches God's Word.

Left Behind

From what I have learned, Jewish boys were taught the scriptures at an early age, somewhere between ages five and six. Since Jesus was born into a Jewish family, it is reasonable to conclude that He was also taught the scriptures at an early age. When Jesus walked the earth, scriptures were handed down from one generation to another verbally. People did not have a Books of Million or a Barnes and Nobles where they could buy their favorite translations of the scripture.

But did Jesus need to learn scripture? Was He not the very scripture that was passed down from one generation to another?

> In the beginning was the Word, and the Word was with God, and the Word was God. He was with God in the beginning. (John 1:1–2 NIV)

> The Word became flesh and made his dwelling among us. We have seen his glory, the glory of the One and Only, who came from the Father, full of grace and truth. (John 1:14 NIV)

The Bible tells us of a time when Jesus's family had been to the temple to worship God. When Mary and Joseph were a day's journey from the temple, they realized that Jesus was not with them. So back to the temple they went. It took them three days to find the twelve-year-old boy, and when they did, they were amazed. There, sat Jesus in the temple's courts with the teachers. But He was not the one who was doing the listening. The teachers were listening to Him and asking Him questions and found that Jesus's understanding of scripture amazing.

> After the Feast was over, while his parents were returning home, the boy Jesus stayed behind in Jerusalem, but they were unaware of it. Thinking he was in their company, they traveled on for a day. Then they began looking for him among their relatives and friends. When they did not find him, they went back to Jerusalem to look for him. After three days they found him in the temple courts, sitting among the teachers, listening to them and asking them questions. Everyone who heard him was amazed at his understanding and his answers. (Luke 2:43–47 NIV)

When Mary saw Jesus, she asked Him, "How could you do such a thing to us? We have been looking for you!" To which Jesus—at the tender age of twelve—answered her,

> "Why were you searching for me?" he asked. "Didn't you know I had to be in my Father's house?" But they did not understand what he was saying to them. (Luke 2:49–50 NIV)

Although Mary may have known that her son was to be the Messiah, her other relatives did not. And because of this, they did not understand how Jesus could have such an understanding of scriptures.

But He did. For He <u>was</u> the Word.

> The Word became flesh and made his dwelling among us. We have seen his glory, the glory of the One and Only, who came from the Father, full of grace and truth. (John 1:14 NIV)

He was the Father. In the words of our Savior,

> "I and the Father are one." (John 10:30 NIV)

Printed in the United States
by Baker & Taylor Publisher Services

—